Absurdly Yours,

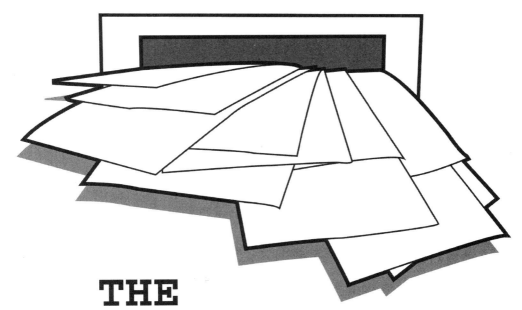

THE

Michael Nugent

LETTERS

BLACKWATER PRESS

CONTENTS

www.michael-nugent.com

*"As long as there are postmen,
life will have zest."*

— William James

DEDICATIONS

To everyone who replied to the letters; to all Nugents, Cotters and Hollidays; to all at Blackwater Press, particularly John O'Connor, Margaret Burns, Paula Byrne and Gary Dermody; to Anne Holliday for the title, Gerard Nugent for the cover and José Nugent for marketing advice; to F Daniel McGuinness MRL URLI, official muse and future author; to all at *Macartacus* and the Limbo lunches for unspecified inspiration; to Carolyn Compelli for supplying the words 'the', 'of', 'to', 'and', 'a', 'in', 'is', 'it', 'you' and 'that'.

MICHAEL NUGENT

Absurdly Yours: The Michael Nugent Letters, 2004
That's Ireland: A Miscellany (with Damian Corless), 2003
Ireland on the Internet: The Definitive Guide, 1995
Dear Me (with Sam Smyth and Arthur Mathews), 1994
Dear John: The John Mackay Letters (with Sam Smyth), 1993

Since time began, Michael has been writing a book about happiness. He has co-written (with Arthur Mathews and Paul Woodfull) a musical comedy play about the Roy Keane and Mick McCarthy misunderstandings in Saipan. He has served time as an Internet 'consultant', a designer, a political and social campaigner, a daytime-television-watching idler, a DIT graduate and an incurable supporter of Bohemians and Leeds United.

© 2004 Michael Nugent

Cover design and photography: Gerard Nugent

Published in Ireland by Blackwater Press,
Hibernian Industrial Estate, Tallaght, Dublin 24

ISBN 1-84131-671-7

Absurdly Yours
THE Michael Nugent LETTERS

PART ONE
POLITICAL PESTERING

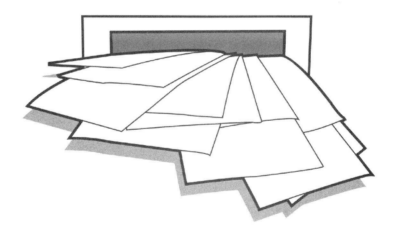

"...In the context of the matters referred to and sought by you, I think it may not be a particular surprise to you that the Tribunal is unable to be of assistance..."

- Judge Michael Moriarty fails to cooperate with a proposed Irish Tribunal Theme Park.

26 July 2004

President Mary McAleese,
Áras An Uachtaráin

Dear President McAleese,

    I am writing a book about international politics and I would appreciate it if you could confirm the accuracy of these paragraphs that I intend to use.

> "In November 1997, Mary McAleese was inaugurated as Ireland's eighth President, and the first from north of the border. She is a qualified barrister, a former Professor of Law and an experienced broadcaster.

> "She is also an able diplomat, with a unique ability to defuse awkward situations. When one prominent Government Minister visited the Áras with a group of constituents, she saw him 'pocket' a valuable silver spoon.

> "Not wanting to publicly embarrass him, she came up with an ingenious solution. Her husband Martin is not only a professional accountant and dentist, but has also for many years performed magic tricks as a party-piece.

> "President McAleese announced an impromptu magic show for her guests. Martin chose the miscreant Minister as his assistant, and asked him to pick a card from a deck. With the Minister suitably distracted, Martin secretly removed the silver spoon from his pocket."

Yours sincerely,

Kelly Shaw

Ms Kelly Shaw

President Mary McAleese,
Áras An Uachtaráin,
Phoenix Park,
Dublin 7

ÁRAS AN UACHTARÁIN
DUBLIN 8

9 August, 2004

Dear Ms Shaw,

Thank you for your letter of 26th July 2004, in which you request confirmation of an event regarding the visit of a Government Minister to Áras an Uachtaráin.

While the information regarding President McAleese in the first paragraph is correct, the remainder of the anecdote has no basis in fact whatsoever.

Should you require any further clarification, I can be contacted at 01 *** ***** or 087 *** ****.

Yours sincerely,

Gráinne Mooney
Personal Executive Assistant

16 July 2004

An Taoiseach,
Mr Bertie Ahern TD,
Government Buildings,
Dublin 2

Dear Taoiseach,

Congratulations on your excellent presidency of the European Union. It made me proud to be Irish. And remember: as Ireland's largest party, Fianna Fáil WON the recent local government elections, regardless of the seedy deals that have since perverted the people's choice.

Now let me explain why I am writing. It is about Lorcan Allen. You know the man: Wexford County Councillor; former Junior Minister; Fianna Fáil National Executive member; admitted to forging your signature on his election material to get ahead of his Fianna Fáil colleague?

Well, my family is from Wexford, and I think I should warn you that I heard from a friend in Gorey that he heard from a former work colleague in Arklow that Councillor Allen is now telling people that it WAS actually your signature on his election literature, and that he had got it by asking you to sign a blank sheet of paper.

I know that this can not be true, but I thought I should let you know anyway. And can you please confirm it to me one way or the other, as I have made a bet with my brother about it.

Yours sincerely,

Hugh Howard

Mr Hugh Howard

An Taoiseach,
Mr Bertie Ahern TD,
Government Buildings,
Dublin 2

Oifig an Taoisigh
Office of the Taoiseach

20 July 2004

Dear Mr Howard,

The Taoiseach, Mr Bertie Ahern, T.D., has asked me to thank you for your very kind thoughts on the outcome of the recent European Council.

The Taoiseach has asked me to say that he feels very proud that so much progress was made during the six months of the Irish Presidency of the European Union.

He thanks you for your support and taking the time to write to him, which he really appreciates.

Yours sincerely,

Fidelma F. Rogers

Fidelma Rogers
Assistant Private Secretary
to the Taoiseach

Telephone: 01-6194030
E-mail: privateoffice@taoiseach.gov.ie

Oifig an Taoisigh, Tithe an Rialtais, Baile Átha Cliath 2.
Office of the Taoiseach, Government Buildings, Dublin 2.

24 April 2004

Mr Micheál Martin TD,
Minister for Health

Dear Minister Martin,

    I live with my elderly mother, who in her anecdotage displays an endearingly mild paranoia. Our doctor assures us it is nothing more serious than the normal passage of time, and we occasionally have harmless family 'in-jokes' at her expense. But it triggered a sensitive predicament when the potassium iodate tablets arrived to protect us from Sellafield.

    Sadly, but unsurprisingly, mother refused to keep the tablets for the proverbial acid-rainy day. Instead, she insisted on taking one, "just in case", on the day they arrived. I stupidly joked that she needed one every day or she would grow an extra head, and I eventually only relieved her irrational panic by convincing her that one a week would do. Yes, I do know it was irresponsible.

    When we ran out, sympathetic neighbours and parish council members started donating us their tablets. They now jokingly call me 'Doctor Glow-in-the-Dark', and I am so familiar with the blessed envelopes that I am the only person in Ireland who knows that they are 'potassium iodate', and not 'iodine'. But Sundays have been heavenly once mother has her weekly tablet.

    However, we have all now run out of tablets, and my workmates seem reluctant to help, so can you please advise where I can bulk-buy potassium iodate tablets, and how much they cost? I want to replace the ones my neighbours have kindly donated, give them the same again as a 'thank you', plus have a sufficient supply on hand to feed mother's harmless habit for the foreseeable future.

    Yours sincerely,

Bernard Campbell

Mr Bernard Campbell

Mr Micheál Martin TD,
Minister for Health,
Hawkins House,
Hawkins Street,
Dublin 2

Office of the Minister

12 July 2004

**DEPARTMENT
OF HEALTH AND
CHILDREN**
AN ROINN
SLÁINTE AGUS LEANAÍ

Quality and Fairness
A Health System for You

Dear Mr Campbell,

Mr Micheál Martin T.D., Minister for Health and Children, has asked me to
thank you for your recent letter concerning potassium iodate tablets.

In the event of a nuclear emergency, iodine tablets offer protection from
radioactive iodine, when associated with other principal countermeasures such
as sheltering and avoiding the consumption of contaminated foodstuffs. The
tablets work by saturating the thyroid gland with stable iodine in order to
prevent it from accumulating any radioactive iodine that has been released into
the environment arising from a nuclear accident.

It should be noted that the pre-distributed iodine tablets are a medicinal product
for use only in the event of a nuclear incident. Persons are reminded not to
exceed the dose as recommended on the packaging. With regard to your current
needs for the tablets, I regret that I am not in a position to source supplies for
your purpose. However, where your mother is concerned, should it not be
possible for you to convince her that she no longer needs these tablets, it is
suggested that you should speak to your local pharmacist with a view to
identifying a placebo that would satisfy her concerns.

I trust that this clarifies the matter for you.

Yours sincerely,

Catherine Burns
Private Secretary

Hawkins House Dublin 2
Teach Haicín Baile Átha Cliath 2
Telephone (01) 635 4000 VPN112
Fax (01) 671 4508

Strangely, the Minister
seems unperturbed that
an entire community has
used up all of their
iodine tablets. But
happily, Mrs Campbell
will now have a placebo
to take when Sellafield
explodes.

11

26 April 2004

The Tribunals of Inquiry,
Dublin Castle, Dublin 2

Dear Mr Justices Mahon & Moriarty,

My Lords, have you seen the musical 'Mary Poppins'? If so, you no doubt start each day singing merrily to yourself as you shave, paraphrasing the stoical Mr Banks from the 'Dawes, Tomes, Mousely, Grubbs Fidelity Fiduciary Bank': "A Tribunal is run with precision; a Tribunal requires nothing less! Tradition, discipline, and rules must be the tools; without them, we have a ghastly mess!"

Then you clock in at the venerable 'Flood-Mahon, McCracken-Moriarty Fidelity Fiduciary Tribunal'. But is there discipline? Is there f*ck! Like Mary Poppins' mad Uncle Albert, the audience floats to the courtroom ceiling from where they cheer or jeer witnesses, laugh at barristers and bay for autographs. Gone is the traditional dignity accorded to Lord Hamilton's Beef Inquiry.

Here is my 'win-win' solution: I and my investors plan to open an Irish Tribunal Theme Park. Our projections show it will be a profitable tourist attraction, while reminding locals of this key period of our history. The material will be presented in an exciting way, thus attracting the more frivolous members of your current audience away from disrupting your work.

We will have daily re-enactments of evidence, floor-shows of the type popular in Disney parks, and interactive booths where people can test their memories. We will also have a permanent display of Tribunal memorabilia, and I enclose a list of the type of items we wish to purchase. How much could we expect to pay? While we will pay top euro for originals, we would realistically be happy with 'Official Replicas Provided by the Tribunals'.

Yours sincerely,

Joseph Williams

Mr Joseph Williams

His Honour Judge Alan Mahon,
His Honour Judge Michael Moriarty,
The Tribunals of Inquiry,
Dublin Castle, Dublin 2

ITEMS SOUGHT FROM THE TRIBUNALS OF INQUIRY FOR
PERMANENT DISPLAY IN TRIBUNAL THEME PARK

- The letter in which Mr Michael Bailey tells Mr James Gogarty that he can "procure planning permission" to have lands rezoned by "procuring a majority vote at two Council Meetings".

- A brown envelope of the type Mr Bailey and Mr Gogarty used a few days later to give between £30,000 and £80,000 to Mr Ray Burke, which was "the equivalent of a nine-inch brick".

- The lists of names supplied by Mr Frank Dunlop outlining the politicians whom he says he bribed; in particular the one in which he amusingly 'outs' Mr Liam Lawlor as "Mr Big".

- The list of places around his house that Mr George Redmond stored his "heavy savings", along with a floor-plan that highlights the kitchen, bathroom, garden shed etc.

- An inflation-adjusted version of the 'price list' for buying broadcasting licences, that Century Radio director James Stafford says was set by Mr Ray Burke and Mr PJ Mara.

- A flow-chart of the relationship between the £50,000 that Mr Tom Gilmartin gave to Mr Padraig Flynn, and the tax-efficient investment schemes run by Beverly Cooper-Flynn.

- The alibi supplied for Mr Bertie Ahern, to prove that he could not have met Mr Tom Gilmartin at the meeting that Mr Ahern later accepted might have happened but was not a meeting.

- The notice distributed in the public gallery, asking people listening to the evidence to "refrain from laughing, clapping and otherwise making unnecessary noise".

- Mr Michael Lowry's offshore account details, along with his Dáil statement that, if he had wanted to hide money from Ben Dunne, he would have opened an offshore account.

- The letter sent by Mr Denis O'Brien to explain that he was too busy to attend to explain that he had only been joking when he claimed to have given Mr Michael Lowry £10,000.

- The false letterheads used by Mr Des Traynor for his illegal offshore accounts, which had Mr Denis Foley "hoping against hope" that he was not an Ansbacher client.

- The letter sent by AIB to new Taoiseach Mr Charles Haughey in December 1979, expressing "every faith in your ability to succeed in restoring confidence in this great little nation".

Tribunal of Inquiry
into Certain Planning Matters and Payments

Appointed by instrument of The Minister for the Environment
and Local Government dated the 4ᵗʰ day of November 1997
as amended by instruments dated the 15ᵗʰ day of July 1998,
the 24ᵗʰ day of October 2002 and the 7ᵗʰ day of July 2003

His Honour Judge Alan P. Mahon S.C. (Chairperson)
Her Honour Judge Mary Faherty S.C.
His Honour Judge Gerald B. Keys

14th July 2004

Dear Mr Williams,

I refer to your letter of the 9th instant (and your earlier letter).

*The Tribunal regrets that it cannot
accede to your request.*

Yours sincerely,

Marcelle Gribbin
Solicitor to the Tribunal

Upper Castle Yard, Dublin Castle, Dublin 2.   Ph: 01-6339800   Fax: 01-6339890   www. planningtribunal.ie

---

Tribunal of Inquiry
(Payments to Messrs Charles Haughey and Michael Lowry)

*Appointed by instrument of
An Taoiseach
dated the 26th day of September 1997
Sole Member:
The Honourable Mr. Justice Michael Moriarty*

Tribunal Office
*State Apartments
The Upper Yard
Dublin Castle
Dublin 2.
Tel: 01-6705666
Fax: 01-6705490*

7th September 2004

Dear Mr Williams,

Thank you for the recent letters sent by you. In the context of the matters
referred to and sought by you, I think it may
not be a particular surprise to you that the
Tribunal is unable to be of assistance.

I take the opportunity of returning the two
stamped addressed envelopes sent.

Yours sincerely

Michael Moriarty

12 July 2004

Mr Michael McDowell TD,
Minister for Justice

cc Garda Commissioner Noel Conroy
cc Censorship of Publications Board

Dear Minister McDowell et al,

I was reading the excellent 'Crime Ireland' magazine when my daughter told me that I was breaking the law. She then showed me this line from her university course notes about the Censorship of Publications Board:

"Periodicals may be prohibited if the Board is of the opinion that they have given an unduly large proportion of space to matters relating to crime."

Don't be silly, I explained. That would mean that Neighbourhood Watch newsletters would be illegal, as <u>all</u> of their space is devoted to matters relating to crime. That's right, she said, but don't worry, sure they just ignore the laws that don't suit them.

I'm not sure if she was talking about the criminals or the Gardaí or the Censorship Board, but this is surely madness. Can you please assist me on how best to refute this argument?

Yours sincerely,

Charles Gray

Mr Charles Gray

Michael McDowell TD,
Minister for Justice,
Department of Justice,
94 St Stephens Green,
Dublin 2

OFFICE OF THE MINISTER FOR JUSTICE, EQUALITY AND LAW REFORM
OIFIG AN AIRE DLÍ AGUS CIRT, COMHIONANNAIS AGUS ATHCHÓIRITHE DLÍ

Dear Mr Gray,

I am directed by the Minister for Justice, Equality and Law Reform, Mr Michael McDowell, T.D., to refer to your correspondence dated 12 July, 2004 regarding the Censorship of Publications Board.

The Minister notes that a similar letter was received in the Censorship of Publications Board recently, to which a reply issued on 30 July, 2004. A copy is enclosed.

Yours sincerely,

Private Secretary

In light of this, the Minister has nothing further to add regarding this matter.

An Garda Síochána

Oifig an Choimisinéara,
An Garda Síochána,
Páirc an Fhionnuisce,
Baile Átha Cliath 8,
Éire.

Office of the Commissioner,
Garda Headquarters,
Phoenix Park,
Dublin 8,
Ireland.

Dear Mr Gray,

I am directed by the Commissioner to refer to your letter of the 12th July, 2004 relative to the "Crime Ireland" magazine. The law relating to periodical publications is contained in the Censorship of Publications Act, 1929 (details included).

It is the view of An Garda Síochána that no offense is committed by the reader of a publication which may be found in contravention of the provisions of Section 7(1) of the Act.

B. CORCORAN
CHIEF SUPERINTENDENT
PERSONAL ASSISTANT
TO COMMISSIONER

OIFIG CHINSIREACHT FHOILSEACHÁN
(Office of Censorship of Publications)

13 SRÁID HAISTE ÍOCHTARACH,
(13 Lower Hatch Street),

BAILE ÁTHA CLIATH 2.
(Dublin 2.)

Dear Mr Gray,

I acknowledge receipt of your interesting letter dated 12 July 2004.

I have not previously heard of "Crime Ireland", which you describe as
excellent and I note that you do not complain of it. I have heard of
"Neighbourhood Watch" newsletters but have not seen them. One assumes
they are periodical publications.

I expect that Section 9(1)(c) of the Censorship of Publications Act 1946:
     "...have devoted an unduly large proportion of space
      to the publication of matter relating to crime"

would in its statutory context be interpreted somewhat as:
     "(in the course of incitement towards commission
      of crimes) have devoted…"

I hope the foregoing will be of some assistance to you with refuting the
argument to which you refer.

The above views are my observations only. Any periodical publication
which is duly complained of would have to be considered by the Board and
dealt with in accordance with the legislation.

Yours sincerely,

Peggy Garvey

Peggy Garvey
Secretary

30 July 2004

All of this seems to
suggest that a magazine
could legally incite
the commission of
crimes, as long as it
did so only within a
small proportion of
space. It would also be
legal to read it.

12 July 2004

Mr Enda Kenny TD,
Leader, Fine Gael

Dear Mr Kenny,

Here's €50 to help build on your success in reviving the party of integrity. I work in the States in brand management. Here is one simple way of adding the party sizzle to the political steak. It is based on research for another product.

A Cincinnati town was once known as "Hamilton" until, in the 1980s, it officially changed its name to "Hamilton!" Yes, with an exclamation mark! Since then, multi-million-dollar investments made "Hamilton!" the "renaissance city of Ohio".

A novel idea, but not entirely original: London's first suffragette play, "The Friend of Women", was a flop. Then in 1907 it became a smash hit when renamed "Votes for Women!" Five years on, English women defiantly marked their ballot papers.

Mr Kenny, this should get you thinking about the branding power of the exclamation mark. And you should ask... why not change the name of the party from "Fine Gael" to "Fine Gael!"? Yes, with an exclamation mark!

Think about it. It works when branding anything. Did hard-nosed traders invest in "Jerry and David's Guide to the World Wide Web"? Not until a multi-million-dollar global brand was created by renaming the company "Yahoo!"

Clearly adding a mere exclamation mark does nothing by itself. But it can form part of a wider strategy. Some political party will be the first to exploit its power. If that party is "Fine Gael!", you may well be the next "Taoiseach!"

Yours sincerely,

George Andrews

Mr George Andrews

Mr Enda Kenny TD,
Leader, Fine Gael,
Leinster House,
Dublin 2

Dáil Éireann	Telephone	Facsimile
Leinster House	01 618 3105	01 618 4502
Dublin 2		E-mail
		Enda.kenny@oireachtas.irlgov.ie

23rd July 2004

Dear George,

Thank you for writing to me recently with your ideas. They are certainly interesting.

On my return from holidays in September maybe we could discuss them further.

Thank you once again for taking the time to write to me and please feel free to keep in touch.

Best wishes,

Yours sincerely,

ENDA KENNY, TD
LEADER OF FINE GAEL

www.finegael.ie

19

26 July 2004

Mr Charlie McCreevy,
Minister for Finance

Dear Minister McCreevy,

My wife and I would like to congratulate you on your promotion to European Commissioner. While we will miss your straight-talking integrity, we know you will do as good a job with the European economy as you have done with ours.

As your fellow commissioners will be jostling for position, you need a 'Big Idea', and we have just the one. It was inspired by the fuss when An Post took ads on postmarks. We were discussing it the other evening and it struck us...

Why not let businesses advertise directly on banknotes and coins? Think about it. Everyone benefits.

The Advertiser: gets their message directly to consumers, at the very moment they are looking at their money. Impulse purchases will soar! Also, businesses can target ads: massive conglomerates can advertise on five-hundred-euro notes; street traders can advertise on coins.

The Consumer: gets better public services, paid for by the ad revenue. Also, you could subsidise the cost of the money itself with some of the ad revenue, so a consumer could buy a ten euro note for nine euro something (we haven't fully worked out the exact details, but you get the idea).

What do you think?

Yours sincerely,

Luke Roberts

Mr Luke Roberts

Mr Charlie McCreevy,
Minister for Finance,
Upper Merrion Street,
Dublin 2

An Roinn Airgeadais
Department of Finance

Oifig an Aire
Office of the Minister

Sráid Mhuirfean Uacht,	Upper Merrion Street,	Telephone: 353-1-676 7571
Baile Átha Cliath 2,	Dublin 2,	Facsimile: 353-1-676 1951
Éire	Ireland	LoCall: 1890 66 10 10
		VPN: 8109
		http://www.irlgov.ie/finance

Our Ref: 04/0606/MF

30 July 2004

Dear Mr Roberts,

The Minister for Finance, Mr Charlie McCreevy T.D., has asked me to thank you for your kind remarks about his nomination for the post of European Commissioner.

As to your suggestion that advertising be permitted on euro notes and coins, this would ultimately be a matter for the European Central Bank (ECB) to decide. However, given the overwhelming need to protect the integrity of the currency and to make it as difficult as possible to produce counterfeit notes and coins, it is most unlikely that the ECB would be prepared to risk the security of the currency by allowing it to carry advertising.

Yours sincerely,

Hannah O'Riordan
Private Secretary

21

24 April 2004

The Managing Directors,
John Player & Sons Ltd,
PJ Carroll & Co Ltd

Dear Sir,

Did you see the weekend papers? The fascist Health-Fuhrers are positively gloating about their success in banning smoking in pubs. We smokers are now Ireland's most persecuted minority. And we are angry. Very angry indeed.

The car-driving clean-air hypocrites may argue that having a smoking area in a pub is as useful as a urinating area in a swimming pool, but that is surely the point - people *do* urinate in swimming pools, but the overall volume of water dilutes it to the extent that nobody notices.

The Health-Fuhrers will never understand the magical interplay between soothing carbon monoxide in our lungs, stimulating nicotine in our bloodstream, and calming alcohol peacefully dulling our senses after a busy day's work.

Shame on them. And, though I do not share Mr Deasy's willingness to break the law, his courage has inspired me to protest against it. I am planning a non-stop public smoke-a-thon outside the Department of Health. I can get a lot of people involved. People who are angry.

Our placards will mix forceful political slogans (such as 'Stop Banning Nature' and 'Most Cancer Is Treatable') with clever wordplay (such as 'John Deasy: A Breath Of Smoke-Filled Air' and 'Minister Martin, Stop Kicking Our Butts').

Could you sponsor this protest by providing the cigarettes? Also, have you any advice for our campaign? We would particularly appreciate if you could send us any pro-smoking statistics or any other information that you think might help.

Yours sincerely,

Richard Roberts

Mr Richard Roberts

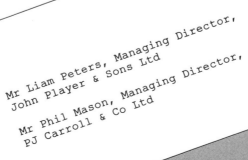

Mr Liam Peters, Managing Director,
John Player & Sons Ltd

Mr Phil Mason, Managing Director,
PJ Carroll & Co Ltd

28 April 2004

Burton Hall Park, Sandyford, Dublin 18, Ireland

Telephone: 01-2052300. Facsimile: 01-2958105

www.pjcarroll.ie

Dear Mr Roberts,

Thank you for your recent letter addressed to Mr. Mason seeking sponsorship for your proposed smoke-a-thon.

In July 2000, the Minister for Health and Children introduced amended regulations under the Tobacco Products (Control of Advertising, Sponsorship & Sales Promotion) Act 1978, which prohibited all sponsorship activities by tobacco companies in Ireland.

As a result we are unable to help you with this campaign.

John Gleeson
Company Secretary

---

5 May 2004

JOHN PLAYER & SONS

56 Park West Road,
Park West,
Nangor Road, Dublin 12.

Tel: +353 (0) 1 243 4800
Fax: +353 (0) 1 243 4801

Dear Mr Roberts,

Thank you for your letter of the 24th April 2004. John Player & Sons is not in a position to sponsor your protest, and indeed any event, as we are prohibited from doing so by Irish legislation.

Regarding your request for statistics, perhaps a useful advocate may be FOREST — a UK based group who advocate smokers' rights.

Information can also be acquired from our parent company website — www.imperial-tobacco.com.

LIAM PETERS
Managing Director

21 September 2004

Ms Mary Harney TD,
Minister for Enterprise,
Trade & Employment

Plus follow-up letter to new
Minister Micheál Martin TD

Dear Minister Harney,

I am writing because I admire the way you stand up for ethical business practices. I have always voted Progressive Democrats and I have never been a member of a trade union.

I work as a sales representative. My group manager has recently completed a 'positive thinking' course in America, and is enforcing some work practices with which I am uncomfortable.

She insists that we start each day by moving our desks against the wall, then linking arms and doing the hokey-cokey dance while taking turns to sing our work targets for the day.

Before we leave, each of us has to hug everyone else for a full minute, while telling them three things they did that day that make us love them more than we did that morning.

This week, we have to stand on our desks while singing our work targets for the day. We don't have to do the hokey-cokey, in case we fall from the desks, but I still think someone might fall anyway.

While sales figures have increased, I really do not like this new regime at all. Is she breaking any employment laws, and is there anything I can do to get her to change?

Yours sincerely,

Frank Allen

Mr Frank Allen

Ms Mary Harney TD,
then Mr Micheál Martin TD,
Minister for Enterprise,
Trade & Employment,
23 Kildare Street, Dublin 2

24

**Department of
Enterprise, Trade
and Employment**

Roinn Fiontar
Trádalá agus
Fostaíochta

Office of the Minister

19 October 2004

Dear Mr Allen,

The Minister for Enterprise, Trade and Employment, Mr Micheál Martin, TD, has asked me to refer to your recent letter to An Tánaiste, Ms Mary Harney TD, regarding your concerns with work practices in your place of employment that you are uncomfortable with. In general, terms and conditions of employment, other than those laid down by employment legislation, are matters for negotiation between an employer and employee.

Unfortunately, there is nothing contained in employment rights legislation administered by this Department to cater for the type of circumstances outlined by you. However, I have detailed below some services of the Labour Relations Commission and Labour Court, both set up under the Industrial Relations Acts, which may assist in resolving your situation.

If, in the meantime matters have not resolved themselves, and you are still uncomfortable with the work practices outlined, you should in the first instance, discuss your concerns with your group manager, individually or as part of a group. If, following this, you are not satisfied with the outcome, you (and perhaps other likeminded employees?) along with your employer, might consider contacting Declan Morrin, of the Advisory Development and Research Service (ADRS) of the Labour Relations Commission (01-6136713). This service works with employers and employees to build and maintain good relationships in the workplace. It enables the parties to develop and implement the means to effectively solve their own problems.

In the event that the above process does still not resolve matters, you, as an individual employee, could consider referring the matter as a dispute with your employer to a Rights Commissioner at the Labour Relations Commission, or to the Labour Court, under the Industrial Relations Act 1969. An explanatory note on the Act and complaint form are enclosed for your information. I am also enclosing a copy of this Department's Guide to Labour Law.

Yours sincerely,

*Bridget Flynn
Private Secretary*

5 October 2004

Pat Rabbitte TD
Leader, Labour Party

Dear Mr Rabbitte,

I have just moved to Dublin from London, where I was active in the New Labour Party. I would now like to get involved with the Irish Labour Party. I don't recommend adopting the title 'New Irish Labour' as you would be abbreviated to the NIL Party. Can you please send me some policy documents: I enclose twenty euro towards the cost of same.

Can I make a suggestion based on our experience in New Labour? When policies become marooned, we use celebrities to attract the attention of a jaded public. Like at our National Conference last week, when our other Tony ('Time Team' Robinson) introduced your great Bono, who memorably described Blair and Brown as the Lennon and McCartney of global development.

Surely there are similar celebrities who could become official spokespersons for the Irish Labour Party? I have asked some of my Dublin friends in the past week, and we compiled the following list: Roddy Doyle on Education, Hector Ó hEochagáin on Foreign Affairs, Brush Shiels on Agriculture, Joe Duffy on Communication, Gerry Ryan on Health and Roddy Collins on Culture and Sport.

While not actually elected, these stars would in effect be the media front-men for your Parliamentary Party. They would appear at press conferences and political television shows, and in 'photo-ops' beside your elected people. Also, if Bono is not available for your National Conferences, one of my friends knows his former colleagues Gavin Friday, Guggi and Dave Id Busaras.

What do you think? It worked for us in New Labour.

Yours sincerely,

Noel Edwards

Mr Noel Edwards

Pat Rabbitte TD
Leader, Labour Party,
Leinster House,
Dublin 2

Pat Rabbitte TD, Party Leader

Dáil Éireann, Leinster House,
Kildare Street, Dublin 2
T: 01 618 3772 / 3980 / 3000
F: 01 618 4032
E: pat.rabbitte@oireachtas.ie
W: www.patrabbitte.ie

6th October 2004

Dear Mr Edwards,

I acknowledge with thanks your letter and comments and I have passed your €20 contribution to Party HQ.

There are no plans to change the name of the Labour Party.

In respect of policy, please check our website as well as the enclosed documents.

Yours sincerely,

Pat Rabbitte T.D.
Labour Party Leader

24 April 2004

Dr Maya Angelou,
Professor of American Studies,
Wake Forest University, USA

Dear Dr Angelou,

You are my favourite poet, ever since your soul-stirring reading at President Clinton's inauguration. I would appreciate your opinion on my latest poem:

MISUNDERESTIMATION

[A poem consisting entirely of phrases used by President George W Bush]

They have misunderestimated me
They have miscalculated me as a leader
Because I know that the human being
And the fish can co-exist peacefully

I am the master of low expectations
But we ought to make the pie higher
We must bring the solution to an end
Before finality has finally happened

But rarely is the question asked:
Is our children learning?
Children living in, you know,
The dark dungeons of the Internet

Why don't you mentor a child to read?
Realize how bright our children is
Then he or her can pass a literacy test
In a literate and a hopefuller country

Yours sincerely,

Gill Weaver

Gill Weaver

Dr Maya Angelou,
Professor of American Studies,
Wake Forest University,
North Carolina, USA

WAKE FOREST
U N I V E R S I T Y

Z. Smith Reynolds Professor
of American Studies

May 24 2004

Greetings!

**Thank you for your informative letter to Dr. Maya Angelou
inviting her to review your poem entitled *Misunderestimation*.**

**Dr. Angelou feels she does not have the expertise to critique
another writer's work, nor does her schedule allow adequate time
to read all the unsolicited poetry and manuscripts received. As
well, due to the proliferation of lawsuits and accusations of
plagiarism in our society, Dr. Angelou has been advised by legal
counsel to refrain from accepting any unsolicited writings, audio
or video tapes.**

**We trust that you understand Dr. Angelou's position in this
matter.**

Sincerely,

Patricia S. Casey
Computer Specialist

Enclosures

P.O. Box 7314, Winston-Salem, North Carolina 27109-7314   (336) 724-0509

10 August 2004

Mr Don Price,
Chief Executive,
National Irish Bank

Dear Mr Price,

I wish to open a new account with your bank. I also wish to express my solidarity with you and your staff in the context of the savage onslaught of the sneering media, who somehow think that it is funny to label you as bank robbers.

So who did you rob? Certainly not your customers. In fact, you assisted them to deal with their finances in a tax-efficient manner. And, unless of course you were dealing with a member of your own family, how would you possibly know whether a customer lived in Castlebar or Camden Town?

Cynics may sneer that you randomly overcharged customers, but the ones you were overcharging were difficult in the first place. So, if you had told them first, there would have been a big debate about what is a fair level of overcharging. You might then have had to overcharge them even more to cover the cost of that debate.

Instead they should (and did) trust you.

And, as a gesture of trust, I would like to transfer some of my funds from their current merchant bank to your good selves. Can you please advise as to the most tax-efficient vehicle in the current culture?

As you're probably watching the cash flow, I enclose ten euro towards the administrative costs of dealing with this query.

Yours sincerely,

George Wilson

Mr George Wilson

Mr Don Price,
Chief Executive,
National Irish Bank,
3 Harbourmaster Place,
IFSC, Dublin 1

Executive Office
International House
3 Harbourmaster Place
I.F.S.C.
Dublin 1
Tel (01) 638 5000
Fax (01) 638 5198

16th August 2004

Dear Mr Wilson,

Thank you for your letter dated the 10th August 2004, to which I am responding on behalf of Mr Price.

We note your position in relation to recent media comment on the affairs of National Irish Bank Limited.

With regard to your query on product offerings from National Irish Bank, I can confirm that National Irish Bank offers a full range of products to suit the needs of both personal and business customers.

It is not clear from your letter if you are seeking information on personal or business products and I would suggest that you contact any branch of National Irish Bank to arrange a meeting to discuss your particular needs.

Alternatively, you may wish to review details of our product range via the National Irish Bank website at www.nib.ie.

Thank you for enclosing €10.00 towards the administrative costs of dealing with your query. I can confirm that we do not require payment for enquiries of this nature and return your €10.00 with this letter.

Yours sincerely,

David Dobson
Senior Manager,
Executive Office

National Irish Bank Limited is regulated by the Irish Financial Services Regulatory Authority
Registered in Ireland Number 65780. Registered Office: 3rd Floor, International House, 3 Harbourmaster Place, I.F.S.C. Dublin 1
A Member of National Australia Bank Group.

3 May 2004

Mr Romano Prodi,
President of the European Commission;
Mr Brian Cowen,
Minister of Foreign Affairs

Dear President Prodi and Minister Cowen,

On Saturday 1st May, European Expansion Day, we held a citizens' conference about expressing the culture of the Union. Our brief was to come up with new, imaginative ideas for you, our decision-makers. Here are our two main proposals.

First, we examined the European Flag. We concluded it should now have 25 stars (one for each state), and that it would be fairer if the stars were of different sizes, based on selected cultural weightings. Our flag design is enclosed. With our formula, Ireland has the biggest star. This is just a coincidence. Using different weightings, any country could have the biggest star.

Next, we heard all 25 national anthems, from the idyllic Czech lyrics (in the garden spring's blossom shines; an earthly paradise) to the French/Irish/UK emphasis on patriotically crushing foes. We concluded that Europe should replace 'Ode to Joy' with an evolving People's Anthem. We suggest that each year's Eurovision Song Contest winner be the European People's Anthem for twelve months.

Think about it: the Union and Song Contest have grown together like Euro-Siamese twins. The Treaties of Rome were signed to the 'Refrain' of Eurovision's first ever winner. The Tokyo GATT round was agreed to 'Hallelujah'. Greenland withdrew while 'Making Your Mind Up'. The Euro notes and coins were celebrated by 'Everybody'. Europe is now expanding 'Every Way That I Can'.

This is our humble contribution as expanding European citizens. Please let us know what you think.

Yours sincerely,

Ger Lindsay

Ms Ger Lindsay,
Secretary

Mr Romano Prodi,
President of the
European Commission,
B-1049, Brussels,
Belgium

PROPOSED NEW
CULTURALLY-WEIGHTED
EU FLAG DESIGN

SUBMITTED TO
MR ROMANO PRODI

NOTE: IRELAND HAS
BIGGEST STAR; IF
USING DIFFERENT
WEIGHTING FORMULA,
ANY COUNTRY COULD
HAVE BIGGEST STAR

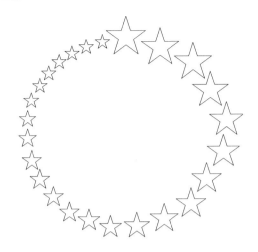

STATES & POLITICAL RANKS BY POPULATION (millions)	Rank	Pop		CULTURAL RANKS BY CALCULATION OF STAR-SIZES (explanations below) Rank	MWP	-SRP	+HSCE	+CCB	= TOT
Ireland	18	4.0	...	1	3.5	2.0	7.5	7	16.0
Sweden	13	8.9	...	2	2.2	3.0	12.2	4	15.4
Greece	8	11.0	...	3	2.6	3.3	5.8	10	15.1
Luxembourg	24	0.4	...	4	1.1	0.7	8.7	5	14.1
Netherlands	7	16.2	...	5	2.6	4.0	11.0	4	13.6
The UK	3	59.3	...	6	3.5	7.7	12.4	5	13.2
France	2	59.6	...	=7	6.0	7.7	8.9	5	12.2
Austria	14	8.1	...	=7	2.3	2.8	11.7	1	12.2
Denmark	15	5.4	...	9	1.7	2.3	10.3	2	11.7
Finland	17	5.2	...	10	1.7	2.3	11.1		10.5
Slovenia	21	2.0	...	11	0.7	1.4	9.7		9.0
Belgium	10	10.4	...	12	2.0	3.2	8.9	1	8.7
Cyprus	23	0.7	...	13	1.1	0.8	7.9		8.2
Czech Rep	11	10.2	...	=14	1.2	3.2	10.1		8.1
Estonia	22	1.4	...	=14	0.8	1.2	7.5	1	8.1
Malta	25	0.4	...	16	0.7	0.6	7.8		7.9
Spain	5	40.7	...	17	3.5	6.4	8.3	2	7.4
Latvia	20	2.3	...	18	0.7	1.5	6.5	1	6.7
Germany	1	82.5	...	19	5.0	9.1	9.3	1	6.2
Hungary	12	10.1	...	=20	1.4	3.2	7.8		6.0
Lithuania	19	3.5	...	=20	0.8	1.9	7.1		6.0
Italy	4	57.3	...	=20	3.8	7.6	7.5	2.3	6.0
Slovakia	16	5.4	...	=20	0.8	2.3	6.8	0.7	6.0
Portugal	9	10.4	...	=20	1.8	3.2	6.3	1.1	6.0
Poland	6	38.2	...	=20	1.9	6.2	6.6	3.7	6.0

MWP	=	Millions of Web Pages with state's name + word 'culture'
-SRP	=	minus Square Root of Population (to nearest thousand)
+HSCE	=	plus % of Household Spending on Culture & Entertainment
+CCB	=	plus Cultural Cohesion Bonuses (+1 for each Eurovision Song Contest victory; +10 to Greece for Plato etc; plus equalisation bonus to ensure each state gets at least 6)

OIFIG AN AIRE GNÓTHAÍ EACHTRACHA
(OFFICE OF THE MINISTER FOR FOREIGN AFFAIRS)

Dear Ms Lindsay,

On behalf of the Minister for Foreign Affairs, Mr Brian Cowen T.D., I wish to acknowledge receipt of your letter of 3 May 2004. Your letter is receiving attention at the moment.

Joseph Hackett

Joseph Hackett
Private Secretary

EUROPEAN COMMISSION
SECRETARIAT-GENERAL

Task Force Future of the Union and institutional questions
TF-A U-2
Institutional matters and governance

Dear Ms Lindsay,

Your letter of 3rd May 2004 addressed to President Prodi, in which you propose a new flag and anthem, has been forwarded to my office.

It was already in 1995 that the **European flag** had been adopted by the Council of Europe. The flag is meant to be a symbol of unity throughout Europe. It is made up by twelve golden stars forming a circle against the background of blue sky. The stars, however, do not represent the number of member states. In fact, their number is invariable, twelve being the symbol of perfection and entirety. At the time of the flag's introduction, the Council of Europe already had more than twelve members. The European Community adopted the European flag in 1986. It is now, since the entering into force of the Maastricht Treaty on November 1st 1993, the flag of the European Union.

The **anthem** was adopted by the Council of Europe in 1972. It subsequently became customary to play it in the Community context as well. On the basis of the proposals formulated by the Adonnino Committee, the Community institutions adopted the anthem at the same time as the European flag (Bulletin of the European Communities No. 4-1986). The European anthem is played without words.

Lars Mitek
Head of Unit

10 September 2004

To: Irish MEPs

Dear *(name of MEP),*

    Well done on getting elected to Europe.

    Is there any chance you could sort me out with two tickets for the Ireland against France game in Paris in October?

    Anywhere in the ground will do. I can sort out the travel myself.

    Thanks a lot,

David Green

Mr David Green

PS Let me know if I can help you with anything.

Liam Aylward, Simon Coveney, Brian Crowley, Proinsias de Rossa, Avril Doyle, Marian Harkin, Jim Higgins, Mary Lou McDonald, Mairead McGuinness, Gay Mitchell, Seán Ó Neachtain, Eoin Ryan, Kathy Sinnott

fine gael

SENATOR JIM HIGGINS

Tel. 6183109
6183764
Fax No. 6184582
E-mail: jim.higgins@oireachtas.ie

Dear David,

First of all, thank you for your good wishes on my election to the European Parliament. As regards the possibility of two tickets for the Ireland v France game in October, I am checking out the situation with the FAI and I'll be in touch with you in due course.

SENATOR JIM HIGGINS MEP

MAIREAD
McGUINNESS

fine gael

Dear David,

Thank you for your good wishes on my election.

Afraid I can't help you with tickets for the match.

Hope you get lucky elsewhere.

Mairead McGuinness, MEP

**Dublin Sinn Fein
58 Parnell Square
Dublin 1**

EUROPEAN PARLIAMENT

MEMBER OF THE EUROPEAN PARLIAMENT

David, a chara,

I refer to your letter of 12 September. Many thanks for your congratulations on my election. Unfortunately I have not been able to source tickets for the match in Paris for either myself or for anyone else. I applaud your resourcefulness in your search for tickets and wish you all the best with it.

Good luck! Is mise le meas,   **Mary Lou Mc Donald MEP**

fine gael *
www.finegael.ie

Euro South Constituency
Simon Coveney TD

Dear David,

Thanks for contacting me and for your good wishes on getting elected to the European Parliament. Unfortunately, I am unable to get any tickets for the Ireland v France game in Paris in October. Renewed thanks and stay in touch.

Simo

Simon Coveney TD MEP

AVRIL DOYLE, MEP

Dear Mr. Green,

Thank you for your letter of congratulations of 12th September and your offer of assistance. Regarding your request for help in obtaining tickets for a France/Ireland match in Paris, I'm very sorry I'm not in a position to help you this time, though my colleagues tell me there should be no problem in getting tickets through the usual channels. I hope you are lucky in your quest.

Avril Doyle, MEP

Marian Harkin TD, MEP

Constituency Office: 1 Dominic Street, Sligo
Tel: 00 353-71-9145888/45890 Fax: 00 353-71-9141973
Email: mharkin@oireachtas.ie

Dear Mr Green,

Thank you for your recent letter. Unfortunately I have no contacts whatsoever in the rugby world. However, if I get an opportunity I will mention it to my French MEP colleagues — I don't know them well, and if I get any positive response I'll let you know.

Orli Bang

Marian Harkin TD, MEP

21 September 2004

Mr Martin Cullen TD,
Minister for the Environment,
Heritage and Local Government

Plus follow-up letter to
new Minister Dick Roche TD

Dear Minister Cullen,

I am a statistician and my wife is a mathematics teacher, and we were talking last night about the electronic voting machines that you ended up not using in the elections.

We assume they must be still lying around in a warehouse somewhere, which is a terrible waste of €50 million of taxpayers' money. So, until you get around to using them, we would like to buy one.

We will use it to teach our children the principles of single transferable voting, by voting as a family on what to have for dinner, what television programmes to watch etc.

That way, when the children reach voting age, they will already be familiar with the machines (you could also sell them to youth clubs or schools for civic classes). Anyway, we have two questions.

- How much do they cost, and would it make more sense for us to buy or rent one? If we buy it, we would of course sell it back whenever you need it.

- Can you confirm that they are programmed in such a way that we can overlay the candidates' names with lists of food groups and television programmes?

Yours sincerely,

Kevin Williams

Mr Kevin Williams

Mr Martin Cullen TD,
then Mr Dick Roche TD,
Minister for the Environment,
Heritage and Local Government,
Custom House, Dublin 1

Oifig an Aire
Office of the Minister

AN ROINN COMHSHAOIL, OIDHREACHTA AGUS RIALTAIS ÁITIÚIL

DEPARTMENT OF THE ENVIRONMENT, HERITAGE
AND LOCAL GOVERNMENT

13 October 2004

Dear Mr Williams,

I have been asked by Mr. Dick Roche, T.D., Minister for the Environment, Heritage and Local Government, to refer further to your recent letter regarding the electronic voting machines. The Minister would also like to convey his thanks for your best wishes on his recent appointment as Minister.

At the outset I would like to point out that, while it was not possible to use the electronic voting and counting system at the June polls, the Government remains firmly committed to the introduction of the system and to securing its benefits at future polls. In this regard, the Government is developing, in consultation with the *Commission on Electronic Voting*, an extensive testing system to address the concerns raised by the Commission's Interim Report.

In relation to your request to purchase or rent a voting machine, I should explain that the voting machine of itself comprises just one element of the electronic voting and counting system. The other key components that make up the system are the *ballot modules* (i.e. bespoke cartridges which are programmed with the election and candidate details), *programme reading units* (which link the ballot module with the election PC and enable the ballot modules to be programmed), dedicated integrated election software and election specific security hardened PCs. The voting machine is used in conjunction with the other constituents of the system and it must be programmed for use by voters using the election software and equipment.

In line with the strict security protocols and safeguards in place with regard to the control of election equipment, and in the interests of the security and integrity of the electronic voting and counting system, it is not considered appropriate to allow either the voting machine hardware or software to be used outside of an electoral or testing environment.

The Minister welcomes your interest in the electoral system. While it has not been possible to accede to your request in relation to the use of a voting machine, please find enclosed a *Guide to Ireland's PR-STV Electoral System*, which the Minister hopes will be of use to you and your family.

Yours sincerely,

Michael Blaa,

PP Cathy Bruton
Private Secretary

24 April 2004

Vice President Richard Cheney,
White House, Washington, USA

Dear Mr Vice President,

I met my dear wife in Wyoming, and her family have always voted for you. Indeed, we had all-night celebrations for your Presidential Medal of Freedom and your ascendancy to the position of Vice President.

Having wed into a Cheney-supporting clan, I follow your lead in investment as well as politics. You have run a Fortune 500 company, from which you earned $35 million in stock options (Al Gore could not count that much, never mind earn it). Since you took the Haliburton helm, my stock has risen with yours, and I unfailingly raise a glass to your health whenever my bottom line expands.

We have only one reservation about this November's election: surely the ticket should be Cheney for President, with Bush as your deputy? Despite his obvious integrity, George W is not the same man as his father. We were relieved four years ago when he chose you to head the committee to recommend his Vice-Presidential candidate, and our relief changed to pride when you became that candidate.

Having represented Wyoming you are familiar with 'Big Nose George', the bungling Pinocchio-featured 19th century train-robber who was buried in a whiskey barrel before the Governor of Wyoming made a pair of shoes out of his skin. Well, as our little family 'in-joke' we affectionately see George W (don't tell him!) as 'Big Nose George' and you, behind the scenes, as the competent Governor capably wearing the real shoes in the White House!

Mr Vice President, could you please send us a signed photo as a memento of your first term?

Yours sincerely,

Thomas Lucy

Mr Thomas Lucy

Vice President Richard Cheney,
Office of the Vice President,
White House, Old Executive Building,
NW Washington, DC 20501,
USA

With best wishes, ~Dick Cheney~

Vice-President Cheney displays his best avuncular smile as he contemplates burying 'Big Nose George' in a whiskey barrel and making a pair of shoes out of his skin.

21 June 2004

High Commissioner Ruud Lubbers,
UN High Commission For Human Rights

Dear High Commissioner Lubbers,

I know you are busy dealing with many problems throughout the world, and that Iraq in particular is very bad at the moment, but in our country a Member of Parliament is being persecuted because he had the courage to stand up for the most basic of human rights.

Defying a draconian ban on smoking in pubs, John Deasy TD smoked three cigarettes in the Members Bar of our Parliament. The fascist Health-Fuhrers responded by sacking him from his job, and banishing him to the political and economic backwaters of Waterford.

This would not have happened in Holland when you were Prime Minister. But there is one place that they cannot put Mr Deasy. To Irish smokers, he is a modern-day Rosa Parks, refusing to be ordered to the designated smoking area for second-class drinkers. And we are angry at his persecution.

Since then, the respected cigarette companies John Player and PJ Carroll have been prevented BY LAW from sponsoring our public smoke-a-thon protest. They have CONFIRMED THIS in writing. And now the fascist Health-Fuhrers have turned their intimidation on the revered human rights campaigner Bono, who smoked a cigarette with Red Hot Chilli Peppers in HIS OWN HOTEL!!!

High Commissioner Lubbers, we the people are angry, and we are getting angrier, if that is possible, on the scale of angriness. Just look at the recent election results!!! How can you help? Can you make a statement supporting the human right to smoke, and calling for the immediate reinstatement of Mr Deasy?

Yours sincerely,

Richard Roberts

Mr Richard Roberts

High Commissioner Ruud Lubbers,
UN High Commission For Human Rights,
Palais de Nations,
8-14 Avenue de la Paix, 1211,
Geneva 10, Switzerland

NATIONS UNIES
HAUT COMMISSARIAT AUX DROITS DE L'HOMME

UNITED NATIONS
HIGH COMMISSIONER FOR HUMAN RIGHTS

Téléfax: (41-22)-917.90.22
Télégrammes: UNATIONS, GENEVE
Télex: 41 29 62
Internet   www.unhchr.ch
Email: tb-petitions@ohchr.org

Address:
Palais des Nations
CH-1211 GENEVE 10

Reference: G/SO 215/51

Geneve, 30 June 2004

Dear Sir,

After careful consideration of the contents of your petition, I sincerely regret having to inform you that the United Nations Office of the High Commissioner for Human Rights is not in a position to assist you in the matter you raise, for the following reason:

> The object of your petition falls outside
> the scope of the relevant treaty.

Accordingly, your petition is being returned to you. You may understand that, while I appreciate your reasons for writing to us, the existing procedures require that it is ascertained whether certain preliminary criteria are satisfied before proceeding with the examination of a petition.

For information about the procedures for the examination of individual petitions on human rights violations, please consult our website: www.unhchr.ch, first click on *ohchr programme*, then on *communications/ complaints*. If you have difficulty accessing our website, write to the UNHCHR, Information Office PW-RS-011, 1211 Geneva 10, and ask for Human Rights Fact Sheets Nos. 7, 12, 15 and 17.

Markus Schmidt
Secretary of the Human Rights Committee

8 September 2004

Éamon Ó Cuív TD,
Minister for Gaeltacht Affairs

Trevor Sargent TD,
Leader, Green party

Dear Minister Ó Cuív and Mr Sargent,

I help to run a youth club. Last weekend we discussed why so few young people speak Irish. The most common complaint was: "You can't text in Irish" (today's youth being more likely to send a text message on their mobile phones than actually speak to someone). "Well now, I bet you can," I challenged. So we spent the next few hours working on an "Irish Texting Dictionary".

We started with basic phonetics and minimising of vowels. For example, "an bhfuil tú" becomes "nwlt". Where numbers (aon, do, trí) are found within a word, you use the numeral itself (1,2,3). For example, "is dócha" becomes "s2ca" (is <u>dó</u>-cha); "cairde" becomes "410" (<u>ceathar</u>-<u>deich</u>); "séipéal" becomes "6pl" (<u>sé</u>-péal); and "seachtain" becomes "7n" (<u>seacht</u>-ain).

Then we moved on to real-life situations. For example, I asked the lads and girls how they would reply if a dangerous stranger sent them this text: "nwlt tr8 cc1 2yl a4a?" ("an bhfuil tú tóraíocht cócaon dóighiúil, a chara?" = are you seeking lovely cocaine, my friend?). One outspoken lad came up with: "mgsdl cccpl" (imigh sa diabhal, cac capaill = go to hell, horse d*ng)!

This all shows the benefits of developing a complete "Irish Texting Dictionary". Irish would 'leap-frog' over other tongues as a modern, relevant youth language. It would also strengthen the case for Irish as an official EU language. Anyway, we're going to run with the idea, and we would welcome any advice or support.

Yours sincerely,

Joseph Phillips

Mr Joseph Phillips

Éamon Ó Cuív TD,
Minister for Community,
Rural and Gaeltacht Affairs

Trevor Sargent TD,
35 Main Street, Swords

An Roinn Gnóthaí Pobail, Tuaithe agus Gaeltachta
Department of Community, Rural and Gaeltacht Affairs

Oifig an Aire
Office of the Minister

Dún Aimhirgín, 43/49 Bóthar Mespil,
Baile Átha Cliath 4, Éire.
43/49 Mespil Road, Dublin 4, Ireland

Teileafón   +353 1 647 3000
Facsuimhir   +353 1 647 3101
E-mail   aire@pobail.ie
Glao Áitiúil 1890 474 847

17 September 2004

Dear Joseph,

Many thanks for your lovely letter of the 8th September 2004, in relation to the possibility of developing the Irish language and making it suitable for texting telephone messages in Irish. I certainly thought the idea was very novel.

I would suggest that you contact Foras na Gaeilge regarding this issue, as issues of dictionary etc. are part of their remit. Foras na Gaeilge is a North/South body, funded jointly by my Department and the Department of Arts, Sport and Leisure in Northern Ireland. Their address is Foras na Gaeilge, 7 Merrion Square, Dublin 2.

You might be interested to hear that my children text me regularly in irish and use some abbreviations; however, their text language is not quite as complicated as the one outlined by you!

Is mé, le meas,

Éamon Ó Cuív T.D.
Minister for Community,
Rural and Gaeltacht Affairs

Trevor SARGENT TD

Party Leader / Ceannaire

Spokesperson on Northern Ireland

Urlabhraí Gaeltachta

Spokesperson on Agriculture & Food

Dáil Éireann
Sráid Chill Dara
Baile Átha
Cliath 2
Éire / Ireland

T 01 618 3465
F 01 618 4524
M 087 254 7836
E trevor.sargent@oireachtas.ie
W www.geocities.com/fingal_green

GREEN PARTY

Comhaontas Glas

DUBLIN NORTH CONSTITUENCY

16th September 2004

Mr Phillips, a Chara,

I am delighted to hear about your innovative project in relation to texting through Irish.

Your local Green party T.D. John Gormley and I generally communicate through Irish, and we will take up your suggestions in the texting area.

I think you are making excellent progress, and if you come across any obstacles let myself or John know.

He can be contacted by phone at 01 618 3019 or fax on 01 618 4597 or on email at johngormley@eircom.net. My own contact details are as below.

Le gach dea-ghuí,

TREVOR SARGENT, T.D.
Party Leader

Home Office:
37 Tara Cove
Baile Brigín
Fingal
Co. Átha Cliath
Fón / Fax (auto): 01 841 2371

Constituency Office:
(above Centra Shop)
35 Main Street
Sord Cholm Chille
Fingal, Co. Átha Cliath
Fón: 01 890 0360
Fax: 01 890 0361

Absurdly Yours
THE Michael Nugent LETTERS

PART TWO

VISONARY VENTURES

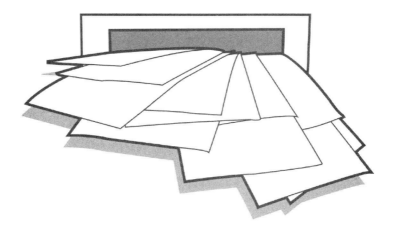

"...I don't think a meeting would be a practical use of our respective time. There is no prospect in the near or medium term future of any aircraft operating with no seats..."

- Michael O'Leary of Ryanair rejects a new partnership.

3 May 2004

Dear Chief Executive,

I am a football fan who works professionally in the field of physics, and I have devised a method to maximise the spin on a ball when bending a free-kick.

A football spins because of the Magnus Effect. The flow of air is faster on one side of the ball, so the different pushes on either side cause it to curve. I am inventing a unique lining (patent pending) for a standard football. To oversimplify, it reformats the gas-filled micro-cells of a Fevernova-style inner syntactic foam.

When the ball is struck, the shape of the lining generates an internal centrifugal force (more technically, an inertial force experienced in a rotating reference frame acting away from the centre of the rotation), which either enhances or counters the curve generated by the outer Magnus Effect.

By changing the direction of the lining's internal spin, we can in effect create either a left-footed football or a right-footed football.

The impact is significant enough for top athletes to gain measurable competitive advantage: certainly on the training pitch, until the lining is officially approved for matches. Please let me know if you would like to see my research.

Yours sincerely,

Robert O'Carroll

Dr Robert O'Carroll

The Chief Executives,
Arsenal FC, Chelsea FC,
Manchester United FC,
The FA, The FAI

Arsenal

ARSENAL STADIUM
HIGHBURY, LONDON N5 1BU

TELEPHONE: (020) 7704 400
FAX: (020) 7704 4001

Dear Dr O'Carroll,

Thank you for your letter dated 3 May. Clearly we operate here with approved footballs.

I have, therefore, sent a copy of your letter to Nike, who may find your research of interest.

K Edelman
MANAGING DIRECTOR

CHELSEA FOOTBALL CLUB

STAMFORD BRIDGE
LONDON SW6 1HS

Phone: 00 44 (020) 7385 5545
Fax: 00 44 (020) 7381 4831
Website: www.chelseafc.com

Dear Dr. O'Carroll,

Thank you for your recent letter regarding the method you have devised to maximise the spin on a ball when bending a free kick.

It was good of you to think of us in this direction but, after consideration, I do not feel that we would wish to pursue your idea.

Peter F Kenyon
Chief Executive

MANCHESTER UNITED

Manchester United PLC, Sir Matt Busby Way, Old Trafford, Manchester M16 0RA

Dear Dr O'Carroll,

It was very interesting reading your proposals. However, I think you would be better placed contacting the Football Association
or a sports manufacturer, as this is
not something that we, as a
club, would pursue.

Thank you for taking the time to write.

Yours sincerely

Philip Townsend
Director of Communications

Patron
Her Majesty The Queen
President
HRH The Duke of York
CVO ADC

The Football Association
25 Soho Square London
W1D 4FA

Telephone
+44 (0)20 7745 4545
+44 (0)20 7402 7151
Facsimile
+44 (0)20 7745 4546

Email
Info@TheFA.com
Visit
www.TheFA.com

TheFA

Dear Dr. O'Carroll,

I write on behalf of Mark Palios in response to your recent letter. The FA is not in the business of football design or production.

We would advise you to approach sports equipment designers with your ideas. Ultimately, any change to equipment has
to be sanctioned by FIFA.

Thank you for taking the time to write
to us and I trust this clarifies our
position.

Jonathan Arana
**Senior Customer
Relations Manager**

Is Mór Linn Peil na hÉireann

Date: 4th May, 2004

Our Ref: FR/JS

Dear Dr. O'Carroll,

I would like to thank you for your letter which I received this morning.

Your research sounds intriguing and I am forwarding a copy of your correspondence to our Technical Director Mr. Packie Bonner.

I note you have a patent pending on your invention and I would like to wish you every success with your venture.

In the meantime if I can be of any further assistance, please do not hesitate to contact me.

pp

Fran Rooney
CHIEF EXECUTIVE OFFICER

THE FOOTBALL ASSOCIA
CUMANN PEILE N
FOUNDE

80 Merrion Sq
Telephone (01) 7037500   F
FAI Homepage: http://w
e.mail: info@fai.ie

Note that Arsenal, Manchester United, the FA and the FAI all seem to have overlooked the disadvantages of trying to play a full football match using a left-footed football.

VISIONARY VENTURE 2
THE DUBLIN BUS

18 July 2004

Dear County Manager,

     I am writing to let you know of my new business venture. Every day, 'The Dublin Bus' will travel around Ireland, stopping in towns to which Dublin Civil Servants have been decentralised, where we will sell, deliver or take orders for Dublin memorabilia. I need to know the following:

- Do we need any licenses to sell food in your County? As well as Dublin editions of newspapers etc, 'The Dublin Bus' will stock sandwiches and rolls made in Dublin that morning, along with contemporary foreign foods and cups of ground-coffee options not usually available outside Dublin, such as lattes and cappuccinos.

- We will create a big-city atmosphere by projecting images onto the sides of local buildings, reminding decentralised civil servants of the DART, the Luas, the Liffey boardwalk, the attractive young people on Grafton Street and the woman who sings on O'Connell Street. Where can we get a list of large plain walls (think big shops, church halls, handball alleys) in small towns in your County?

- We will also rent 'The Dublin Bus' to stag/hen parties for country trips. Where are the best places in your County for people who, to put it bluntly, just want to get very drunk? As a responsible company, we will liaise with local publicans and Gardaí, provide a condom machine on the bus, and provide a sober driver to transport the revellers back to Dublin after their festivities.

Yours sincerely,

Alex McCabe

Mr Alex McCabe

To: County Managers
in Counties to which
Dublin Civil servants
may be decentralised

LAOIS COUNTY COUNCIL
COMHAIRLE CHONTAE LAOISE

July 27th 2004

Dear Mr. McCabe,

I refer to your letter of the 18th July 2004 and wish to confirm that the sale of food is subject to licence and is regulated in general by the Health Boards. In the case of County Laois, you should contact the Midland Health Board, Arden Road, Tullamore, County Galway. Laois County Council is not aware of any large plain walls referred to by you. You would need to source them yourself and consult with owners.

In relation to your query relating to parties, I confirm that such an approach will be resisted by this Council and the promotion of such activities need to be referred to the local Gardaì. I am sending a copy of your letter and this reply to the local Garda Superintendent for his information and attention.

Louis Brennan
Deputy County Manager

WEXFORD: I wish to acknowledge receipt of your letter addressed to the County manager dated the 18th July 2004. The contents of your letter have been noted.

MEATH: With the limited information given, it is difficult to say that the planning process will not apply, so contact should be made with the Planning Department with actual specifics. The proposal may also require a Casual Trading licence and a Health Board permit.

DONEGAL: At the May Council meeting the following exemptions were incorporated into the Donegal County Casual Trading General Bye Laws 2004: (1) To exempt the selling of hot food by touring Hot Food Vendors provided that they do not remain static for a period exceeding four hours at any one stop and they do not trade within 100 metres of any commercial premises trading in hot food, between the hours of 20.00 and 19.00 hours; (2) To exempt the selling of ice cream by touring Ice Cream vendors which do not remain static for a period exceeding four hours at any one stop. If your venture falls within the above exemptions, you will not require a Casual Trading licence.

Comhairle Chontae Chill Mhantáin
WICKLOW COUNTY COUNCIL

Aras An Chontae,
Cill Mhantáin.
Telefón : (0404) 20100
Fax No : (0404) 67792
E-Mail: manager@wicklowcoco.ie
Web: www.wicklow.ie

28th July 2004

Dear Mr McCabe,

I refer to your letter of the 18th inst. regarding your proposed new business venture. The Government decision on 'decentralisation' allocated only 140 jobs from the National Standards Authority of Ireland to be located to Arklow, County Wicklow. We are extremely disappointed with this allocation and, from your point of view, it may not create the scale of demand which would make your business viable in County Wicklow. Nevertheless both Wicklow County Council and Arklow Town Council will do everything possible to make the transferees feel welcome and to help integrate them into the local community.

Wicklow is a very cosmopolitan County and has all the advantages of being close to Dublin without the disadvantages of being part of Dublin. Instead of the congested streets, polluted atmosphere and atrociously high prices of Dublin, transferees to Arklow will enjoy the benefits of proximity to wonderful places such as Brittas Bay and Glendalough, relatively inexpensive housing and cheaper grocery prices with a better overall quality of life. I understand that some Arklow residents already have access to fine foods including lattes, cappuccinos and fresh sandwiches and rolls.

Your suggestion of projecting Dublin images onto buildings in small towns in County Wicklow would really not be appropriate as they would be visually obtrusive and would detract from the quality environment with which this County of ours has been blessed. This part of your proposal may well raise a number of other issues including planning requirements, avoidance of light pollution and impact on the welfare of farm and domestic animals etc.

I am absolutely confident however that exposure to the mountains, lakes, valleys, rivers and coastal areas of Wicklow will vastly improve the lifestyles of the transferees and that any residual hankering after the images which you have mentioned will disappear quickly. I have noticed many attractive young people on the streets in Wicklow and even an occasional female street singer.

contd...

...contd.

As a member of the board of Wicklow Tourism, I can advise you that the attraction of visitors to the County who as you so bluntly put it "just want to get very drunk" is not a particularly high priority in our marketing plan for the County. Having seen the noise, the anti-social behaviour, the public urinating and vomiting caused by some such parties in Temple Bar, it strikes me that they are really more suitable for larger cities, which have the facilities and the services which can support and cope with them.

There are of course many fine pubs in Wicklow where we encourage the sensible use of alcohol (and incidentally most of them are quite progressive and have condom machines) and these contribute to the overall quality of life experience which we provide to residents and visitors.

I hope that the above has been helpful. Can I as chairman of Wicklow County Enterprise Board also suggest that you may need to carry out some Market Analysis of the likely demand from the potential transferees to Arklow for the goods and services which you mentioned in your letter? This would be particularly important if you need to prepare a business plan to support a funding application to a bank or other financial institution. I also note from recent media coverage that there is likely to be a delay in relation to the Government's decentralisation programme and this may have an impact on the positive cashflows which could accrue from your project.

Finally, I think that you should consider visiting our County to experience at first hand the wonderful amenities and ambience which will already be available to your potential customers, and this may help you to fine tune any "added value" which could be provided by your "Dublin Bus" project.

Yours sincerely,

EDDIE SHEEHY
WICKLOW COUNTY MANAGER

**VISIONARY VENTURE 3
CELTIC & RANGERS
FOR PEACE**

22 September 2004

Dear friend,

This is a wonderful week for Northern Ireland. My wife
and I were delighted to hear the Rev Ian Paisley saying that we
are closer than ever before to solving the problems that have
plagued us all. We both thought that, at this pivotal point in
time, we should consider imaginative ways to help everyone go
the extra mile. So here is what we have come up with.

As you know, sport has amazing power as a symbol of
friendship. Think of the Olympic Games, and the World War
Christmas Day football matches. Sadly, with Northern Ireland,
sport has acquired a negative symbolism because of the intense
rivalry between Glasgow Celtic and Glasgow Rangers. But, we
wondered, what if we were to use that power for good instead of
evil?

So here is our idea: for one football season, a
consortium of Irish and nationalist public figures would sponsor
Glasgow Rangers, and a consortium of British and unionist public
figures would sponsor Glasgow Celtic. In all of their
competitive games during the sponsored season, Rangers would
display a tricolour on their shirts and Celtic a Union Jack.

The sponsors would also host fundraising events, with the
money going to support the peace process; the Rangers one would
be held on Saint Patrick's Day, and the Celtic one on the 12th
of July. To strengthen the symbolism, and add a positive
religious dimension, the Queen of England and the Pope would be
joint patrons of both of the sponsorship consortiums.

What do you think? Would you support such an initiative?
And what advice would you have to help make it a reality?

Yours sincerely,

Peter Madden

Mr Peter Madden

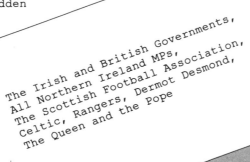

The Irish and British Governments,
All Northern Ireland MPs,
The Scottish Football Association,
Celtic, Rangers, Dermot Desmond,
The Queen and the Pope

UlsterUnionists

Simply British

Dear Mr. Madden,

Thank you for your correspondence, the content of which has been most informative and I should inform you that I have noted the same.

Yours sincerely,

PP Rt. Hon. David Trimble MP MLA

Cunningham House	**Tel**	028 9076 5500
429 Holywood Road	**Fax**	028 9076 9419
Belfast BT4 2LN	**Email**	uup@uup.org

www.uup.org

OIFIG AN AIRE GNÓTHAÍ EACHTRACHA
(OFFICE OF THE MINISTER FOR FOREIGN AFFAIRS)

BAILE ÁTHA CLIATH 2
(DUBLIN 2)

Dear Mr. Madden,

On behalf of the Minister for Foreign Affairs, Mr Dermot Ahern T.D., I wish to acknowledge receipt of your letter of 4 October regarding football sponsorship in Northern Ireland. Your letter is receiving attention at the moment.

Yours sincerely,

**Cyril Brennan
Private Secretary**

> Memo to the Department of Foreign Affairs: Glasgow is not "in Northern Ireland".

10 DOWNING STREET
LONDON SW1A 2AA

From the Direct Communication Unit   **4 October 2004**

Dear Mr. Madden,

The Prime Minister has asked me to thank you for your recent letter. Mr Blair is grateful to you for letting him have your views, which he was interested to see.

Yours sincerely,

SUSAN JAMES

BUCKINGHAM PALACE

Dear Mr. Madden,

The Queen has asked me to thank you for your letter of 22nd September expressing your feelings regarding the steps being taken to create a more peaceful Northern Ireland, and offering your own proposal for promoting religious tolerance within the community. Her Majesty understands your reasons for writing as you did and has taken careful note of your comments.

As a constitutional Sovereign, the Queen acts on the advice of her Ministers, and I have, therefore, been instructed to send your letter to the Right Honourable Paul Murphy, MP, the Secretary of State for Northern Ireland, so that he may know of your approach to Her Majesty on this matter and may consider the points you raise.

Yours sincerely,

Mrs. Sonia Bonici
Senior Correspondence Officer

GERRY ADAMS MP
Uachtarán Shinn Féin

25th October, 2004

Peter a Chara,

Thank you for your letter of 22nd September 2004. First let me apologise for the delay in responding.

I agree with you that sport is a great way of bridging the divide. However, I am unsure of how you would put your plan into action as you may encounter objections causing further division.

I wish you well with your endeavours and would appreciate if you would keep me updated if your initiative gets off the ground.

Is mise le meas,

Paula Mac Inams
PP

Gerry Adams MP

13 July 2004

Dear President,

I am dealing with the Department of Education about my plan for a visionary new Irish educational institute. Imagine a teacher doing this roll-call: Allen, Woody; Bach, Seb; Einstein, Albert; Gates, Bill... Our teacher will be bored long before reaching McSharry, Ray. Why? All are academic 'failures'. My new institute will celebrate such successes. It is the University of Real Life, Ireland (URLI). Its slogan: 'The URLI Bird Watches The World.'

URLI will have no syllabus: Students will pay their fees, then spend their week doing whatever they would have been doing anyway (real life). Every Saturday, they will attend tutorials. The guest speaker can be anyone from a tycoon to a tramp, with experience of real life but no academic qualification. Tutorials will have no set format: people can do whatever they think is most useful.

Tutorial fees will make URLI self-financing. Students will accumulate credits to graduate with a DipRL (Diploma in Real Life), BRL (Bachelor of Real Life) or MRL (Master of Real Life). The guest speakers will decide how many credits, if any, each student gets. The criteria are arbitrary, reflecting real life. Sometimes fair, sometimes not. Live with it. Learn from it. Real life.

While celebrating the absence of formal qualifications, URLI will also honour the pursuit of traditional degrees as an equally valid life choice. To reflect this, I plan to hire tutorial rooms in existing Universities, including yours. Could you please send me details of cost etc? Also, as a more formal association, would you be interested in URLI operating as a Faculty of Real Life within your University?

Yours sincerely,

Bill Stevens

Mr Bill Stevens

The Presidents of
TCD, UCD, DCU, UL, UCG and
Maynooth, Queen's and Ulster
Universities.

Dear Mr. Stevens,

Thank you for your letter of 13th July 2004, which awaited my return from an out-of-country trip.

In accordance with your requests, I am enclosing the room rates charged for the academic year 2003/4. The contact person and her coordinates are indicated on the form. I regret that the University of Limerick is not interested in establishing a Faculty of Real Life at this time. However, I wish you every success in your interesting and innovative venture.

UNIVERSITY *of* LIMERICK

OLLSCOIL LUIMNIGH

With warm regards,

Roger GH Downer
President

National University *of* Ireland, Galway
Ollscoil na hÉireann, Gaillimh

Dear Mr. Stevens,

Dr. O' Muircheartaigh has asked me to forward a copy of our room hire rates to you, which I am now enclosing. Wishing you every success with your venture.

Kind regards,

Anne Duggan
Conference Manager

UNIVERSITY OF ULSTER: From Gerry McKenna, Vice-Chancellor and President. Thank you for your letter of 13 July. I note your proposals. The University has no interest in becoming involved at this time.

QUEEN'S UNIVERSITY: The Vice-Chancellor has asked me to acknowledge receipt of your letter of 13 July 2004. While recognising that there have been many people who have achieved a great deal without the benefit of a University education, our position is that a university education should be available to all those who can benefit from it. It would be incongruous if the University were to be seen to support an organisation which extolled the virtues of education through life's experience. I regret therefore that we are unable to assist you.

16 July 2004

Dear Minister O'Donoghue et al,

Self Aid was a defining moment for 1980s Ireland. What other national event could have united the Boomtown Rats, Bagatelle, Ruairi Quinn, Moving Hearts, Paul Brady, AnCO, the Chieftains, the Pogues, the Youth Employment Agency, Van Morrison, Clannad and the National Manpower Service? But where are they all today?

The shameful truth is that society has neglected most of these musical patriots whose integrity and altruism exceeded even their talent. Did you see the recent documentary with former Bay City Roller Les McKeon trying to buy shopping with green shield stamps? Well, his plight is mild compared to many Self Aid icons.

I personally know a bass guitarist who still spends most of his dole money on Actifed, a drummer who was hospitalised with clinical depression after he failed to be accepted for seven FAS courses, and a gifted singer whose only musical release is chanting obscenities at Shamrock Rovers matches. I have heard many similar stories, the heartbreak of which I could not begin to convey.

Yes, of course U2 have done very well. And yes, Elvis Costello recently played the North Sea Jazz Festival. And others have forged new careers outside music: Brush Shiels and Christy Moore are now regular guests on the Joe Duffy and Late Late Shows, while Chris de Burgh manages his daughter's modelling career. But who can even speculate on what happened to Big Self, Blue in Heaven, Les Enfants, the Fountainhead and Those Nervous Animals?

Frankly, we have let them down. So I am seeking your support and advice in planning a national fundraising event, 'Self Aid Aid', to help repay the forgotten Self Aid performers for their gift to Ireland almost twenty years ago.

Yours sincerely,

Christy Doran

Mr Christy Doran

John O'Donoghue, Minister for Arts, Sport & Tourism; Arts spokespersons of other parties; AGSI, ICTU

Department of Arts, Sport and Tourism
An Roinn Ealaíon, Spóirt agus Turasóireachta

Office of the Minister
Oifig an Aire

6th August 2004

Dear Mr Doran,

Further to your recent correspondence to John O'Donoghue TD, Minister for Arts, Sports and Tourism, I advise that I have passed your correspondence to Mr. Ultan Waldron, Private Secretary to Mr. Tom Kitt TD, Minister of State at the Department of Foreign Affairs, for his attention and direct reply to you on this matter.

Department of Arts, Sport and Tourism
An Roinn Ealaíon, Spóirt agus Turasóireachta

Office of the Minister
Oifig an Aire

3rd September 2004

Dear Mr Doran,

I wish to refer further to your recent correspondence to John O'Donoghue TD, Minister for Arts, Sports and Tourism, and to my response dated 6th August 2004, in which I informed you that your correspondence was forwarded to the Department of Foreign Affairs for their attention. In the meantime, I have been informed that your query does not fall within the remit of that Department. I would like to take this opportunity to apologise for any inconvenience caused.

In any case, I must inform you that there is no funding available to this Department to assist with your proposal. I am sorry that I cannot be of assistance on this occasion. However, if I can be of assistance on any other matter please do not hesitate to contact me.

Yours sincerely,

Thérèse O'Connor
Private Secretary

Approx. translation:

John O'Donoghue: "Hey, hasn't Tom Kitt's son got something to do with music?"

Department of Foreign Affairs: "Yes, but you're not getting us to do your job."

Jimmy Deenihan, TD, MCC
Finuge
Lixnaw
Co. Kerry

DÁIL ÉIREANN
BAILE ÁTHA CLIATH, 2.

Tel.:   068-40154/068-40235
Fax: 068-40383
E Mail: jdeenihan@eircom.net
Tel.:   01-6183352 (Dáil)
Fax: 01-6184145 (Dáil)

Dear Christy,

Thank you for your letter of July 16th. My apologies for not replying earlier. Regarding the fundraising event, I am sure that if the top personalities in the music business supported it, it would be a great success. I will be back in Dublin in two weeks if you should wish to contact me at (01) 6183352.

Yours sincerely,

Jimmy Deenihan, T.D.

Fine Gael Arts Spokesperson

Jack Wall TD

DÁIL ÉIREANN
BAILE ÁTHA CLIATH, 2.

Castlemitchell, Athy, Co. Kildare
Tel: (059) 8631495 (home)
087 2570275 (mobile)
01 6183571 (Dáil) Fax: 01 6184638
E-mail: jack.wall@oireachtas.ie

Dear Christy,

Further to your letter in regard to artists that have hit on bad times, I obviously share your concerns in regard to your friends and indeed many others who are in such situations. I have raised this matter on a number of occasions with the Minister and with our spokesperson on Social and Family Affairs Mr. Willie Penrose TD. We have also met with SIPTU in regard to this matter. I would certainly be willing to meet you in regard to discussing this matter and I would be grateful if you could contact me to arrange a meeting in Leinster House.

Yours sincerely,

JACK WALL TD.

Labour Party Arts Spokesperson

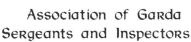 

Association of Garda Sergeants and Inspectors

Cumann Sairsintí agus Cigirí den Gharda Síochána

Dear Mr Doran,

I refer to your letter of 16th July 2004. I note that you are planning a national fundraising event based on the 1986 Self Aid concert in the RDS and that you are seeking members of AGSI to provide policing services free of charge on the day.

The provision of policing services is a matter for the local District Officer in which the event is to take place. Neither my Association nor I have any function in this. As your event is to take place in the RDS, might I suggest that you contact the District Officer at Donnybrook Garda Station and discuss your plans with him. I hope that I have been of some assistance to you on this matter.

Pat Flynn
General Secretary

CONGRESS
WORKING FOR PROGRESS

IRISH CONGRESS OF TRADE UNIONS

Dear Mr. Doran,

I wish to acknowledge receipt of your letter of 16 July regarding your national fundraising event.

Unfortunately, Congress is not in a financial position to assist with this and is restricted to sponsoring Congress activities only.

Yours sincerely,

David Begg
GENERAL SECRETARY

8 September 2004

Dear City Manager,

I have been contracted by a newly formed lobby group to produce a website to promote rural living. This new group has prominent patrons, and will soon be formally launched. The website will include a downloadable video that we have recently shot, which includes urban footage from your area.

In it, a rural family visits a city. The film is speeded up and has a humorous soundtrack. They enjoy the tourist attractions and shopping centres, but hate the litter-strewn streets and cold, rude, zombie-like city-dwellers. We then go to slow motion as the family leaves, but gets caught up in an interminable traffic jam. The rest of the video portrays the joys of rural life: clean air, healthy living, natural foods, friendly neighbours etc.

Arising from this, we have two questions.

- Some of our film footage was shot inside public facilities, such as libraries, courthouses and rubbish dumps. Do we need permissions to run with these scenes on the Internet and, if so, where should we apply?

- When filming the traffic jam scene, we were lucky enough to capture a road-rage incident. Nobody was badly injured. But it gave us an idea. Do you have any closed-circuit TV feeds of dangerous areas of your city which we could link into for a live feed on the website? Naturally, we will pay.

Yours sincerely,

Dick Riordan

Mr Dick Riordan

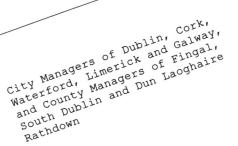

City Managers of Dublin, Cork, Waterford, Limerick and Galway, and County Managers of Fingal, South Dublin and Dun Laoghaire Rathdown

COUNTY **COUNCIL**

Comhairle Chontae Dhún Laoghaire - Ráth an Dúin

Our mission is to provide a quality Local Government service for all our citizens and customers

Dear Mr Riordan,

I wish to acknowledge receipt of your letter dated 8th September, 2004.

I have referred the matter to Ms. Therese Langan, Senior Executive Officer, Corporate Services Department, for examination and reply.

Yours sincerely,

Derek Brady
County Manager

Comhairle Contae Fhine Gall
Bosca 174, Áras Contae, Sord, Fhine Gall,   Tel: (01) 890 5000
Contae Átha Cliath.

Fingal County Council   Tel : 8905153
P.O. Box 174, County Hall, Swords, Fingal,
Co. Dublin.   emer.coleman@fingalcoco.ie

Dear Mr Riordan,

Thank you for your letter of 8th September. We note your request with regard to the use of footage shot in Fingal.

In order for us to respond, you will need to send us a copy of the video or web address where we can download a copy.

We will then let you know the situation.

Yours sincerely,

Emer Coleman
Communications Officer

3 September 2004

Dear County Manager,

I wrote to you six weeks ago about operating a new business venture in your County. The response from other Counties has boosted our early confidence, and we are also in touch with Dublin Bus regarding branding possibilities.

However, we really need nationwide data to finalise our business plan. That said, I appreciate your understandable delay in responding. Indeed, it opens up the possibility of a 'win-win' situation.

You are clearly busy running an entire County without the basic administrative resources with which we are familiar in Dublin.

This bodes well for 'The Dublin Bus', which will bring a new level of efficiency into the County on a regular basis. And you can in turn use this positive development to argue for more resources from Central Government.

As I say, 'win-win'.

Meanwhile, I enclose a stamped addressed envelope towards the administrative costs of responding to my original questions.

Yours sincerely,

Alex McCabe

Mr Alex McCabe

To County Managers who did not reply to the first letter about The Dublin Bus project

CLARE COUNTY COUNCIL
Comhairle Chontae an Chláir

20th September 2004

Dear Mr. McCabe,

I refer to your letters of the 3rd September and of the 18th July to the County Manager. I must apologise for the delay in responding to same. The Council does, of course, welcome new business ventures particularly where they benefit Clare.

The sale of food from your proposed Dublin Bus could have a number of implications particularly from an environmental health point of view, traffic safety and obviously the impact on the local business community who are paying rates to Clare County Council. There is also the requirement for a license under the Casual Trading Act. I would point out that many of the ground coffee options indicated in your letter are, in fact, available locally and have been for some time now.

I do not see any difficulty in identifying suitable locations to project images onto the sides of local buildings. You already mention places such as church halls, handball alleys, community facilities etc. I would suggest that considerable research is needed before you embark on the venture, including likely take-up. I am unsure if you have undertaken market research in the area. However, the Council does wish you well with your business venture.

Gerard Dollard,
Director of Services
Economic Development & Planning

WESTMEATH: I wish to acknowledge receipt of your correspondence in relation to operating a new business venture in County Westmeath. I wish to advise that I have referred the matter to Mr Hugh O'Reilly, Senior Executive Officer, Corporate Affairs, who will respond directly.

SLIGO: I wish to acknowledge receipt of your letters and I regret the delay in replying to you. Enclosed is an application form and copies of bye laws in relation to casual trading in County Sligo. As you propose to sell food you would also need to contact the North Western Health Board, Markievicz Road, Sligo.

(Enclosed: 10 pages of application forms and bye laws.)

Louth County Council
Comhairle Chondae Lughaí
"Opening doors to a brighter future"

15th Sep 2004

Dear Mr. McCabe,

I am in receipt of your correspondence dated 3rd September 2004. I have no record of receiving your previous correspondence dated 18th July 2004.

Sale of food from a 'bus' would require authorisation in accordance with the Casual Trading Act and also Health Board clearance. You may be surprised to know that a number of the items which you mention, e.g. foreign foods, lattes, etc., are readily available in provincial towns around Ireland, including the towns in Louth.

While your expectation of projecting images onto buildings to create the Dublin City atmosphere may be interesting, I can assure you that towns in Louth have their own unique and attractive character and heritage and would be surprised if any building owners were happy to accommodate your proposal. However, perhaps your best route would be to visit some locations and carry out some direct market research.

In relation to your final suggestion regarding the 'Dublin Bus', I would suggest that you contact the Vintners Federation of Ireland.

Martina Moloney
County Manager

 KERRY: I acknowledge receipt of your letter of 3rd September, 2004. I wish to advise that this matter has been referred to Mr. Brendan O'Connor, Administrative Officer, Roads and Transportation.

 CARLOW: I have been asked by the County Manager to refer to your letters of 3rd September and 18th July. In relation to your queries:

- Food licensing is a matter for the South Eastern Health Board.
- Commercial opportunities (large blank walls etc): you might wish to visit to see the town yourself.
- Perhaps on your visit to Carlow you might visit the local pubs, which I am assured provide good Carlow and Dublin beers.

25 April 2004

Dear Mr O'Leary,

Good luck with your new Charleroi agreement. Your reluctance to dip into my pockets for your profits contrasts with my constant dread of the Aer Lingus anti-trade unions. I would appreciate your opinion on a concept in my doctoral thesis, 'Comfortably Profitable: Ergonomics and Economics in the Aviation Industry'.

The idea arose when I spent a flight in Uzbekistan sitting on a wooden crate filled with live chickens, after take-off was delayed while the pilot did a 'whip-around' to buy fuel. Since then I have often wondered: do airplanes really need seats? I know they are traditional but, financially, they waste the 'unused' space above the lap of each passenger and below the luggage bins.

I am now examining a concept called 'lean-backs': equivalent to seats but without the part that you sit on.

Visualise a row of backward-leaning L-shaped person-height dominoes, reclining at an angle that balances comfort with retention of the overhead bins. Another (adjustable) angle towards the base accommodates bending of the knees. The feet rest on a spongy material capable of absorbing the impact of landing. The passengers are safely strapped in.

Mr O'Leary, I would appreciate your opinion on 'lean-backs', in the form of a quote that I could include in my thesis.

Yours sincerely,

Pierce Whitehead

Mr Pierce Whitehead

Mr Michael O'Leary,
Chief Executive, Ryanair,
Dublin Airport,
County Fingal

Corporate Head Office
Dublin Airport
County Dublin
Ireland
Telephone: +353 1 8121212
General Fax: +353 1 8121213
Telex: 33588 FROP EI
Sita: DUBHQFR
Reservations: Ireland 0818 303030
            U.K.:   0871 2460000
            Website:www.ryanair.com

Department Fax Numbers:
Finance: 01 8121330
Sales & Marketing: 01 8121331
Flight Operations: 01 8444404
Engineering: 01 8121338
Reservations: 01 6097901

Ab/MOL/6126

29th June 2004

Dear Mr Whitehead,

I thank you for your recent letter, but regret that we simply cannot meet the crazy number of requests that we get from students doing theses/ dissertations/projects.

It would be invidious to select some but not all of these requests, and we find it simplest and less offensive to do none.

I hope you understand and wish you every success with your project.

Yours sincerely,

Adele Bannon
Assistant to the Chief Executive

Ryanair Ltd.
Registered in Ireland No. 104547

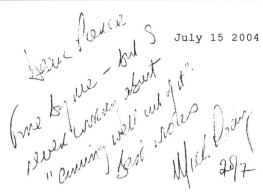

Dear Pierce
Fine by me — but I
never worry about
"coming well out of it".
Best wishes
Mick O'Leary
29/7

July 15 2004

Mr Michael O'Leary
Chief Executive, Ryanair,
Dublin Airport,
County Fingal

Your Ref: Ab/MOL/6126

Dear Mr O'Leary,

    Thank you for your recent reply to my request for a quote for my thesis on ergonomics and economics in the aviation industry. I fully understand your position as outlined in your letter. I have drafted the following as a 'win-win' compromise:

> "I next contacted Mr Michael O'Leary, whose economic sense and visionary approach to ideas that challenge conventional industrial wisdom I have always admired, and who has single-handedly dragged the European aviation industry into putting the consumer first.
> Thank you, Michael.

> "While the Ryanair Chief Executive amusingly proclaimed himself plagued by crazy requests from students doing theses, his tone could in no way be regarded as either invidious or offensive. What came to my mind was his playful smile as he mocked the policy paralysis of successive governments.

> "And, while the maverick multi-millionaire did not directly comment on the novel concept of 'lean-backs', nor did he rule them out as an integral part of the future of the aviation industry. He closed our exchange by wishing me every success with the project. I appreciated his good wishes."

    How does that sound? I think you come well out of it, without committing yourself to anything.

    Yours sincerely,

Pierce Whitehead

Mr Pierce Whitehead

Letter returned with this handwritten note:
"Dear Pierce, fine by me. But I never worry about 'coming well out of it'. Best wishes, Michael O'Leary."

The Reverend W. Martin Smyth, M.P.

(Belfast, South)

HOUSE OF COMMONS

LONDON SW1A 0AA

Tel: 020 - 7219 4098
Fax: 020 - 7219 2347
Email: tearleg@parliament.uk

Reply to
117 Cregagh Road
Belfast BT6 0LA
028 - 9045 7009
Fax: 028 - 9045 0837

27th September, 2004

Dear Mr Madden,

Thank you for your letter of 22nd September.

I was glad that you and your wife were delighted to hear the Rev. Ian Paisley saying that we are closer than ever before to solving the problems here. However, the news coming out at the moment is not that inspiring.

I am fascinated by your imaginative suggestions. I am aware of course that at the World War Christmas Day football matches the Germans did not play on the British side and the British certainly did not support the German side.

However, sometimes we actually magnify the negative symbolism between these clubs. We have it in Northern Ireland between Linfield club and Glentoran club, and virtually every other team wants to bash Linfield or if Glentoran is at the top they want to beat them.

I would suspect that for one football season it would be seen primarily as a gimmick. It would be interesting to discover how many of the business folk who are in that position to support these things would go down that road.

Yours sincerely,

W. Martin Smyth, MP

Dermot F Desmond
Chairman

28th September, 2004

Dear Mr Madden,

Thank you for your letter of September 22nd.

I think that your solution is a very creative one but unfortunately too extreme for implementation.

Nevertheless, it is people like you that will ensure that sometime in the near future we have full harmony on this little island of ours.

Thank you for your thoughtfulness.

With kind regards,

Yours sincerely,

Dermot F. Desmond

International Investment & Underwriting Limited
IFSC House, Custom House Quay, Dublin 1. Tel +353-1-605444. Fax +353-1-6700400

75

ALDERMAN PETER D ROBINSON MP MLA

Tel No: (028) 9047 3111

Fax No: (028) 9047 1797

HOUSE OF COMMONS
LONDON SW1A 0AA

Please reply to:

**Strandtown Hall
96 Belmont Avenue
Belfast, BT4 3DE**

Our Ref: PDR/CN/22,715
29 September 2004

Dear Mr Madden,

Thank you for your letter dated 22 September 2004. We are indeed, in the Democratic Unionist party, hopeful that devolved government can be established at Stormont with all the parties concerned committed to exclusively peaceful democratic means and accountable institutions.

I have read with great interest your imaginative ideas for using football to symbolise friendship. I have a considerable number of reservations. I imagine getting support from all the various interests involved would prove extremely difficult. It would be interesting to know how the particular clubs would respond to your idea as so much income is derived from shirt sales.

In any event, best wishes with your project.

Yours sincerely

PETER ROBINSON MP, MLA

28th September, 2004

Ref: 1760/G/C/03

HOUSE OF COMMONS
LONDON SW1A 0AA

Dear Mr Madden,

Thank you for your letter regarding a football initiative involving Glasgow Celtic and Glasgow Rangers.

While I would support in the long term your suggested initiative, these things have to be worked out very gradually, with both sets of participants feeling comfortable with the proposition, and at this moment it would be premature.

GREGORY CAMPBELL MP

---

28 September 2004

HOUSE OF COMMONS
LONDON SW1A 0AA

Dear Mr Madden,

Thank you very much indeed for your recent correspondence which I read with interest. I have had an occasion to correspond with both Celtic Football Club and Rangers Football Club in the past. This arose out of my concern that in North Belfast in particular groups of rival kids and youths came out to riot wearing the football jerseys associated with each of the clubs. When I contacted the clubs they pointed me to the strong anti-sectarian programmes and projects which they have in place. I was wondering, therefore, whether or not you had made contact with the clubs as I think it would be important to get them on board before any further initiative was taken.

NIGEL DODDS OBE MP MLA

3 September 2004

Dear President,

I wrote to you on 13 July about the University of Real Life, Ireland (URLI). Since then the venture has advanced: several University campuses are ready to go and the Minister for Education is making relevant inquiries.

However, I really need nationwide data to finalise my business plan. Time and tide wait for no bank manager. And in the real world, outside the ivory prefabs of academia, seven weeks is more than enough time in which to expect a reply to a letter.

I assume the delay is due to 'cuts' in your budget. Thankfully, students do not protest about these any more. Such attention-seeking is a good precursor to working in the media or Dáil Éireann, but it chips little from the coalface of commerce.

So here is a practical solution: I would like to tender for a contract to provide administrative back-up to your office. I can supply people who will, on your behalf, reply to ALL of your letters within three working days, EVEN in summertime. Real life.

Meanwhile, I enclose a stamped addressed envelope to cover the cost of replying to my initial queries.

Yours sincerely,

Bill Stevens

Mr Bill Stevens

The Presidents of the universities who did not reply to the first letter: TCD, UCD, DCU, Maynooth and UCC.

President's Office
University College Cork, Ireland

**Oifig an Uachtaráin
Coláiste na hOilscoile
Corcaigh, Éire**

8 September 2004

Dear Mr Stevens,

I write to acknowledge receipt of your letter of 3 September 2004, addressed to the President, Prof. G.T. Wrixon. As you know, Prof Hyland, Vice-President, addressed your queries in her letter of 13 July 2004 (copy attached) but it appears that the letters crossed in the post.

President's Office
University College Cork, Ireland

*Vice-President: Professor ¡ ine Hyland
Med, PhD, HDE*

**Oifig an Uachtaráin
Coláiste na hOilscoile
Corcaigh, Éire**

30 August 2004

Dear Mr. Stevens,

I note with interest your plan to establish a "visionary new Irish educational institute" and I wish you every success with your plan.

While UCC is open to applications for rental of classroom space on campus, you are probably aware that in common with some other higher education institutions in this country, classroom space is at a premium in UCC.

During term time it is quite impossible for us to consider applications from outside groups as we cannot even provide space on campus for our own students. Every year we have to rent teaching space off-campus to accommodate all our students. I am sorry I cannot be of more help to you at this time.

Yours sincerely,

Áine Hyland
Vice-President

UNIVERSITY OF DUBLIN

TELEPHONE (353 1) 608 1558
FACSIMILE (353 1) 608 2303
E-MAIL provost@tcd.ie

PROVOST'S OFFICE
TRINITY COLLEGE
DUBLIN 2
IRELAND

Dear Mr Stevens,   7 September 2004

The Provost would like to thank you for your letters of 13 July and 3 September, which he read with interest. He has passed your letters to the Senior Lecturer, Professor John Murray, for his attention. Professor Murray oversees the academic programme for the College and is best placed to answer your queries. He will respond to you directly over the coming weeks.

Regarding the lack of response to your first letter, please accept my apologies. This was due to an administrative mix up in the Provost's Office and we sincerely regret any inconvenience this may have caused you.

Caitriona Curtis
Administrative Officer

UNIVERSITY OF DUBLIN   TRINITY COLLEGE

EDUCATION DEPARTMENT
3087 ARTS BUILDING
TRINITY COLLEGE, DUBLIN 2

Dear Mr Stevens,   29 September 2004

The Provost has referred your letter of 13th July to me. Unfortunately, pressure of work with further travel and conference presentations have prevented an earlier response, so I apologise for my delayed response. Your intriguing, and somewhat humorous, letter is certainly worthy of serious consideration. Perhaps the best way to address it would be on three levels: practically, theoretically and spatially.

Practically, what you suggest is interesting in a contemporary Irish context. The current Minister for Education has made a sustained attempt to address issues of equality and access for third level institutions, so you would be pursuing the correct path by maintaining contact with the Department. Two other organisations that may be relevant to you are the Further Education and Training Accreditation Council (FETAC) and the various VECs around the country.

contd...

...contd.

FETAC offers ways of progressing learners, particularly those who may not have progressed through matriculation, into further education and towards recognised certification. Part of their work allows some scope for developing Level 2 Modules and there may be room within that scope for an educationally sound 'Unit of Study in Real Life' — to paraphrase from your letter.

As the various VECs around the country offer many post-compulsory and further education classes leading to FETAC certification, there may be an appropriate context for your suggestions to be realised. The VECS are very strong in local and community education sectors, and this is where your letter seems best situated. Thus to contact both groups may be in your interest.

Theoretically, perhaps there are two significant issues your letter seeks to address. The first is pedagogical, while the second is epistemological.

- It would appear that the pedagogical foundation for your project is perhaps not so strong. Would all invited tutors be considered equally? If your criteria for awarding credits is arbitrary, is the selection of tutors also arbitrary? Both pose problems pedagogically, as such a seemingly random selection of tutors (i.e. 'from a tycoon to a tramp') would ignore the significant role of educational skills that teachers must have. Likewise, if credits were awarded in an openly arbitrary manner, what significance would the award be? Both of these factors would indicate that your proposal may lie outside the formal university setting.

- From an epistemological perspective, what you are offering is an approach seemingly based on 'standpoint epistemology'. However, a reading of such an epistemological framework would require some form of value be attached not solely on experience, but the understanding and articulation of that experience. This would not be based on 'criteria [which] are arbitrary', but would be based on some explicit value judgement. Again, such a position, if properly construed, would place your project outside the formal university setting.

Spatially, and from a more practical perspective, perhaps there is one third level institution in Ireland working along the lines that you suggest: Saor-Ollscoil na hÉireann (Free University of Ireland) at 55 Prussia Street, Dublin 7. To conclude, it would seem that in the current context it would be difficult for Trinity College to adopt your project. However, in pursuing some of the suggestions above, you may find an appropriate context.

Yours sincerely,

Mona O'Moore.

Professor Mona O'Moore
Head of Department of Education

17 July 2004

Dr Alan Westwell,
Managing Director, Dublin Bus

Dear Dr Westwell,

I am writing to let you know of my new business venture, and to ask a few questions about our potential relationship. We already have our own bus, called 'The Dublin Bus'.

'The Dublin Bus' will travel around towns with decentralised civil servants. We will sell Dublin memorabilia and audio tapes of shows from Dublin radio stations. In our video-tape booth, civil servants can buy taped messages from Dublin-based relatives, and record messages which we will bring back to Dublin. At weekends we will rent 'The Dublin Bus' to stag and hen parties.

Obviously, our names sound alike. So we have two suggestions.

- One: 'Dublin Bus' could sponsor 'The Dublin Bus' (We have other sponsors, but you could have top billing).

- Two: we could use a typeface that highlights the word 'THE' in our name, thus avoiding confusion between 'Dublin Bus' and 'THE Dublin Bus'. We could even use a tagline like 'Not <u>A</u> Dublin Bus; <u>THE</u> Dublin Bus'.

We are of course also open to any suggestions you have. We do not want to get off on the wrong footing. Please let us know what you think. We look forward to hearing from you.

Yours sincerely,

Alex McCabe

Mr Alex McCabe

Dr Alan Westwell,
Managing Director,
Dublin Bus,
59 Upper O'Connell Street,
Dublin 1

82

Bus Átha Cliath

Bus Átha Cliath/Dublin Bus
59 Upper O'Connell Street,
Dublin 1.
59 Sr. Uí Chonaill Uachrarach
Baile Átha Cliath 1
Tel: +353 (01) 872-0000
Fax: +353 (01) 873-1199
Web: http://www.dublinbus.ie

July 20, 2004

Dear Mr McCabe,

I write to acknowledge receipt and to thank you for your letter, dated 17th July, on behalf of Dr. Westwell.

Our Business Development Manager, Mr. Paddy Doherty, will respond in detail next week once he returns from annual leave.

Siobhan FitzMaurice
Secretary to the Managing Director

Bus Átha Cliath

Bus Átha Cliath/Dublin Bus
59 Upper O'Connell Street,
Dublin 1.
59 Sr. Uí Chonaill Uachrarach
Baile Átha Cliath 1
Tel: +353 (01) 872-0000
Fax: +353 (01) 873-1199
Web: http://www.dublinbus.ie

cc Mr Paddy Doherty

Dear Mr McCabe,

First of all may I congratulate you on your forward thinking with regards to decentralisation. However, I have to point out to you that Dublin Bus is a registered trade mark belonging to us and cannot be used by anyone else.

I have sent a copy of your letter to our solicitors who will give you the exact legal position. I suggest in the meantime that you look at another name and the best of luck with the venture.

Bronagh Rooney,
Marketing Manager.

3 September 2004

Dr Alan Westwell,
Mr Paddy Doherty,
Ms Bronagh Rooney,
Dublin Bus

Dear Dr Westwell, Mr Doherty and Ms Rooney,

Thank you for your series of cc'd letters in response to mine of 17 July regarding 'The Dublin Bus', which will travel around towns with decentralised civil servants selling Dublin memorabilia.

We accept your suggestion that we consider another name instead of 'The Dublin Bus'. We have had a workshop around this theme, and would like to run the following proposals by you:

- 'The Dubh Linn Bus'. This is our favourite. It sounds like Dublin Bus, but it isn't. Also, your Irish version is 'Bus Átha Cliath' so there should be no confusion.

- 'Dublin or Bust'. This would kindle the natural desire of decentralised civil servants (indeed, any Dubliners living down the country) to buy Dublin memorabilia.

- 'The Dublin Puss'. Our logo would be a pussy cat in the style of Bus Éireann's red setter.

Would any of these be acceptable? As we will both be in almost the same line of business, we do not want to upset Dublin Bus in any way. We are also open to any suggestions you have.

Yours sincerely,

Alex McCabe

Mr Alex McCabe

Dr Alan Westwell, Managing Director; Mr Paddy Doherty, Business Development Manager; Ms Bronagh Rooney, Marketing Manager; Dublin Bus

Bus Átha Cliath

Bus Átha Cliath/Dublin Bus
59 Upper O'Connell Street,
Dublin 1.
59 Sr. Ui Chonaill Uachrarach
Baile Átha Cliath 1
Tel: +353 (01) 872-0000
Fax: +353 (01) 873-1199
Web: http://www.dublinbus.ie

September 7, 2004

Dear Mr McCabe,

I write to acknowledge receipt and to thank you for your letter, dated 3rd
September.

We are considering its content and will
respond further in due course.

Dr. Alan R. Westwell
Managing Director

Bus Átha Cliath

Bus Átha Cliath/Dublin Bus
59 Upper O'Connell Street,
Dublin 1.
59 Sr. Ui Chonaill Uachrarach
Baile Átha Cliath 1
Tel: +353 (01) 872-0000
Fax: +353 (01) 873-1199
Web: http://www.dublinbus.ie

September 13, 2004

Dear Mr McCabe,

Thank you for your letter of 3rd September re the branding of your bus service.

I am afraid that the name of 'The Dubh Linn Bus' has already been registered
following a radio promotion with Gerry Ryan.

With regard to the other names, there is nothing
we can say, in that it could not work as a joint
venture arrangement, but the best of luck with
the venture.

Bronagh Rooney
Marketing Manager

4 October 2004

Dear City Manager,

I know you are a busy man, so my apologies for interrupting your work with this follow-up letter, but I wrote to you a month ago, on September 8 (copy enclosed) seeking some information about a video that we are producing for a forthcoming website.

I have tried explaining to our rural colleagues that, in the clinical and impersonal environment of city life, it is not unusual for large organisations to simply ignore letters from ordinary people. However, while facing such discourtesy is now second nature to me, my clients are from parts of the country where people interact with each other on a daily basis.

Their unrealistic expectations of a reply are now putting me under pressure: I have meetings next week on Wednesday 13 October with the lobby group regarding video editing, and on the following day with their (again, rural) bank manager regarding the business plan, and their legal people insist that we have any required permissions in place before these meetings.

Can you please oblige? I would be extremely grateful.

Yours sincerely,

Dick Riordan

Mr Dick Riordan

The City Managers who did not reply to the first letter: Dublin, Cork, Waterford, Limerick and Galway, and County Manager of South Dublin

Comhairle Cathrach Luimneach   **Limerick City Council**

Dear Mr Riordan,

I refer to your letters of 4th October and 8th September. The answers to your questions are:

1. You do not have our permission to use the film footage you refer to.
2. We cannot assist you in this matter.

Apologies for not replying sooner.

Yours sincerely,

T. Mackey

Tom Mackey

City Manager

Comhairle Cathrach Chorcaí Cork City Council

CITY HALL
CORK

Fón/Tel: 021-4924000
Faics/Fax: 021-4314238
Líonra/Web: www.corkcity.ie   Ref

Dear Mr Riordan,

I refer to your letter of 4th October, 2004, in relation to a video you have produced and your request for clearance to use scenes from Cork City.

I would be obliged if you would contact Mr. Damien O'Mahony, our Communications Officer, with whom you can discuss the issue. Mr. O'Mahony can be contacted at 021 4924134.

J. GAVIN
CITY MANAGER

Dublin City Council
Comhairle Cathrach Bhaile Átha Cliath

Office of the Assistant City Manager, Environment & Culture
Department, Civic Offices, Wood Quay, Dublin 8, Ireland

Dear Dick,

Regrettably we are not in a position to provide you with C.C.T.V. footage because of personal and privacy considerations.

Equally any footage of City Council Facilities that contains images of staff or the public cannot be used for the same reason.

Yours sincerely,

Philip Maguire,
Assistant City Manager.

SOUTH DUBLIN COUNTY COUNCIL
COMHAIRLE CHONTAE ÁTHA CLIATH THEAS
CORPORATE SERVICES DEPARTMENT
County Hall, Town Centre, Tallaght, Dublin 24

Dear Mr Riordan,

The County manager has referred your letter of 4th October, 2004 to me for reply. There is no record of your letter of 8th September, 2004 being received by the County manager. It is policy and indeed practice that all correspondence received by the County manager is acknowledged and recorded.

The Council's permission is required prior to the taking of any images, video, film, photographic, etc. on Council owned property. Subject to prior approval being received it would be permissible to use the images obtained on your website. The Council does not have any closed circuit TV imagery of dangerous places as defined under Local Government (Sanitary Services) Act 1964.

Mary Whitney
Administrative Officer
Corporate Services Department

WATERFORD CITY COUNCIL
COMHAIRLE CATHRACH PHORTLÁIRGE

CORPORATE AFFAIRS DEPARTMENT
The Mall, Waterford
Telephone: (051) 309900   Fax: (051) 879124

11 October, 2004

Dear Mr. Riordan,

I refer to your letter of the 8th October 2004.

Before any consideration can be given to the matter, the City Council requires the following:

(a)   The name, composition, constitution, articles and memorandum of the group you represent.

(b)   Full contact details of the group, including the names and addresses of the principals, directors and/or committee.

(c)   A copy of the video you propose to use.

Waterford City Council believes that living, working and doing business in, and visiting Waterford City is an extremely positive experience and would not wish to be associated with any anti-City promotional interest.

Yours sincerely

Paddy Power
Deputy City Manager

8 September 2004

Dear Bishop,

Ever since my husband and I saw poor Father Horan interrupt the marathon in Athens, we have been wondering how to restore the good name of Irish priests in the minds of Olympic fans everywhere. Then last night the perfect idea dawned on us.

We holidayed in Spain this July, where we saw the 'Running of the Bulls' in Pamplona. As you know, this is a festival in memory of the town's first bishop, Saint Fermin. The bulls are raced through the town, and everyone has a party.

While it was exciting, it was marred for us by the fact that the bulls were killed at the end of it. But what if we had a more humane version of this Christian festival in Ireland? So here is our idea: an annual 'Running of the Priests' festival.

This would be an ecumenical event, where bishops, priests and ministers of all denominations, wearing their full clerical garb, would race through a different Irish town or village each year while being cheered on their way by locals and tourists alike.

It has the Christian connotations of Pamplona without any of God's creatures being harmed, AND would bring thousands of tourists to Ireland, AND would change the world's current negative linkage of Irish priests and athletics to a new positive one.

There would be no 'competitive' edge to the race; it would be in the spirit of the Dublin marathon, but with bishops and priests and ministers of all ages. What do you think? And would you be interested in getting involved?

Yours sincerely,

Joan Byrne

Mrs Joan Byrne

Roman Catholic and
Church of Ireland
Bishops and Archbishops

The Bishop of Limerick & Killaloe

THE RIGHT REVEREND M.H.G. MAYES

13/09/2004

Dear Ms Byrne,

Thank you for your letter of the 6th September. On the lighter side, I don't think you would want to see me running anywhere, with or without robes — the spectacle would be too much for most spectators who would die of heart attacks brought on either by laughter or terror.

The only time I ever won a race was nearly sixty years ago when I fled from an angry policeman with drawn revolver who had caught me throwing stones at windows. I had previously asked him what they did to boys who broke windows, and he said "first of all we shoot them, then we hang them and finally we drown them", which was a singularly terrifying catalogue of punishments indeed.

Happily, I have reached an age where I can decline all invitations to run anywhere without being a spoilsport. If you do persuade any of the more athletic clergy (and/or Bishops?) to take part, I might come along to take photographs.

On the more serious side concerning the killing of God's creatures, I'm not sure what to make of that, especially since we do it all the time on a massive scale. Our economy depends on it. Just visit the nearest butcher's shop.

Whether Pamplona is more cruel than what goes on in an abattoir depends a great deal on whether the bulls know what lie in store for them. I understand that a skilled matador can dispatch a bull very quickly indeed, which means that not much suffering is involved, or at least no more than the animals experience in the "human" environment of the abattoir.

With all good wishes,

Yours sincerely,

Bishop of Limerick and Killaloe

Bishop's House, North Circular Road, Limerick.
Telephone: 061 +451532 (from R.I.), +353+62+451532 (from other countries) Fax: 061 451100
email: bishop@limerick.anglican.org

**Archbishop's House,
Tuam,
Co. Galway**

Telephone: (093) 24166 Fax: (093) 28070

Email: archdiocesetuam@eircom.net

Dear Mrs. Byrne,

Archbishop Neary has asked me to convey his sincere thanks to you for your letter to him of the 8th September 2004.

I am to say that, while the Archbishop does not regard your remarkable suggestion as being entirely practicable, he is deeply impressed by the imaginative scope involved.

He sends you his warmest good wishes.

Yours sincerely,

Rev. Brendan Kilcoyne
Diocesan Secretary

From the office of the Most Rev Dr John W Neill, Archbishop of Dublin and Bishop of Glendalough, Primate of Ireland and Metropolitan:

Dear Mrs Byrne, I acknowledge receipt of your letter of the 8th September and shall bring it to the Archbishop's attention.

From the office of the Most Rev Seamus Hegarty, Bishop of Derry:

Dear Mrs Byrne, I am in receipt of your letter addressed to Bishop Hegarty. Bishop Hegarty is out of the country at present but I shall bring your letter to his attention on his return later this month.

From the office of the Most Rev Philip Boyce, Bishop of Raphoe:

Dear Mrs Byrne, I wish to acknowledge receipt of your letter to Bishop Philip Boyce. The Bishop is away at present. Be assured that I will bring the contents of your letter to his attention on his return.

Ara Coeli, Cathedral Road
Armagh BT61 7QY

Telephone 028 3752 2045
Fax   028 3752 6182
(Country Code 44)

Email admin@aracoeli.com
www.armagharchdiocese.org

Dear Mrs Byrne,

On behalf of Archbishop Brady, I write to acknowledge your letter of 8 September 2004.

Please be assured that the Archbishop is giving careful attention and consideration to the matters you
have raised in your letter.

With kindest regards,
Yours sincerely,

(Mrs.) Úna Kennedy
Secretary

Tel: (051) 874463.
Fax: (051) 852703.
Email: waterfordlismore@eircom.net
Website: www.waterfordlismore.com

**BISHOP'S HOUSE,
JOHN'S HILL,
WATERFORD.**

Dear Mrs Byrne,

I wish to acknowledge your letter to me of 8th September 2004.

I am afraid I wouldn't be interested in getting involved.

My kindest regards and my good wishes,

Yours very sincerely,

**William Lee,
Bishop of Waterford and Lismore**

August 10 2004

Dear Mr O'Leary,

I am delighted that you have started to actively promote the seat-free airplane concept, and I would like to arrange a meeting to see how we can develop it further as a joint venture partnership. I have now added the following to my thesis:

"Mick O'Leary (our thinking is so similar that I now feel that we are almost friends) then showed how quickly he can react to a positive concept. I first contacted him in April with the then-novel proposal that airplanes might not need seats.

"In May he told Der Spiegel that: 'You could have airplanes with no seats, in ten years' time. Why do you have to sit down?' In August *The Sunday Times* wrote that '[O'Leary] talks of an airline in which reclining seats have gone; maybe one day there'll be no seats at all.'

"I tipped a wink to this great innovator, who had taken my embryonic idea and quickly cast it loose in the marketplace of aviation ergonomics. I looked forward to the day when we signed on the dotted line and began to exploit it commercially."

How does that sound? Please let me know when would be a good time for us to discuss the idea further. As you are more experienced in these matters, I would be happy to discuss whatever proposal you may have about the nature of our partnership.

Yours sincerely,

Pierce Whitehead

Mr Pierce Whitehead

Mr Michael O'Leary,
Chief Executive, Ryanair,
Dublin Airport,
County Fingal

Corporate Head Office
Dublin Airport
County Dublin
Ireland
Telephone: +353 1 8121212
General Fax: +353 1 8121213
Telex: 33588 FROP EI
Sita: DUBHQFR
Reservations: Ireland 0818 303030
U.K.: 0871 2460000
Website:www.ryanair.com

Department Fax Numbers:
Finance: 01 8121330
Sales & Marketing: 01 8121331
Flight Operations: 01 8444404
Engineering: 01 8121338
Reservations: 01 6097901

Ab/MOL/8040

11th August 2004

Dear Mr Whitehead,

I thank you for your letter of 10th August, and wish you continued success with your thesis.

Unfortunately, we don't engage in joint venture partnerships, I haven't started to promote the concept, and I don't think a meeting would be a practical use of our respective time.

There is no prospect in the near or medium term future of any aircraft operating with no seats. In fact, Ryanair is presently investing in upgrading our seats to market leading body contoured, all leather covered units designed to maximise the comfort and safety of our passengers.

Best wishes,

Michael O'Leary
Chief Executive

Ryanair Ltd.
Registered in Ireland No. 104547

September 12 2004

Mr Michael O'Leary
Chief Executive,
Ryanair

Dear Mr O'Leary,

Regarding our discussions of airplanes with no seats, I've now made a scale model of a sample cabin interior.

It comes in three pieces, each four feet long. You can clip it together very easily, and lift up one wall to see the interior. I'd love to show it to you, but transporting it is a problem.

Luckily, I have a friend in furniture removal, and he can lend me his van very early next Tuesday morning (21 September) to bring it over. He will collect it again on the Wednesday of the following week any time after 7 pm.

So I will bring it over early on Tuesday, and I can stay around the airport all day doing other research until you are free to meet me. Or if you would rather examine the model first, I can leave it and call back another day.

Whatever suits your schedule will work for me. If you are not around on Tuesday 21st, where would be the best place for me to leave the model?

Yours sincerely,

Pierce Whitehead

Mr Pierce Whitehead

Mr Michael O'Leary,
Chief Executive, Ryanair,
Dublin Airport,
County Fingal

Corporate Head Office
Dublin Airport
County Dublin
Ireland
Telephone: +353 1 8121212
General Fax: +353 1 8121213
Telex: 33586 FROP EH
Sita: DUBHQFR
Reservations: Ireland 0818 303030
U.K.: 0871 2460000
Website:www.ryanair.com

Department Fax Numbers:
Finance: 01 8121330
Sales & Marketing: 01 8121331
Flight Operations: 01 8444404
Engineering: 01 8121338
Reservations: 01 6097901

Ab/MOL/9050

14th September 2004

Dear Mr Whitehead,

I thank you for your letter dated 12 September and refer you to my previous letter of 11 August (copy enclosed).

Regrettably we have no interest in your concept and therefore no interest in a meeting.

Yours sincerely,

Michael O'Leary
Chief Executive

Ryanair Ltd.
Registered in Ireland No. 104547

4 October 2004

Dear President,

I wrote to you on 13 July and on 3 September about the University of Real Life, Ireland (URLI). We have had an overwhelming response from potential students. Over the coming weeks, before we formally start our tutorials, we plan to bring some of our students to existing universities to establish a comparative frame of reference.

Next week we plan to visit UCD on Wednesday, DCU on Thursday and Maynooth on Friday. We will be there all day. There will be up to a hundred of us, ranging in age from 17 to 82. We will include: plumbers, electricians, zoo staff, bus drivers, street entertainers, single parents with children, motivational speakers, waiters, rehabilitated drug addicts and at least one retired fishmonger.

We will break into smaller groups and sit in at the backs of random lectures, asking difficult 'real-life' questions of the lecturers, such as: 'How do you know that?' and 'How many jobs would that create?'. By doing this, we will test both the flexibility and relevance of the formal academic environment. We will require canteen seating at lunchtime. At least twenty of us will require vegetarian options. We can provide extra canteen staff if needed.

We will call to reception to announce our arrival. Perhaps you could have someone there with photocopied maps of the campus, and the day's timetable for various courses? We will pay for these. This should be an interesting day for all involved. Is there anyone we should talk to in advance to fine-tune our schedule?

Yours sincerely,

Bill Stevens

Mr Bill Stevens

The Presidents of the universities who did not reply to the first two letters: UCD, DCU, NUI Maynooth.

Corporate and Legal Affairs Secretary's Office, Room 128A
Michael Tierney Building, Belfield, Dublin 4, Ireland

Oifig an Rúnaí Corporáideach agus Gnóthaí Dlíthiúla, Seomra 128A
Áras Mhíchíl Uí Thiarnaigh, Belfield, Baile Átha Cliath 4, Éire

Tel: +353 1 716 1458/1411   Fax: +353 1 716 1162
E-mail: john.coman@ucd.ie

University College Dublin

An Coláiste Ollscoile, Baile Átha Cliath

Corporate and Legal Affairs Secretary's Office

Oifig an Rúnaí Corporáideach agus Gnóthaí Dlíthiúla

7 October 2004

Dear Mr Stevens,

I refer to your letter of 4 October. We are happy to welcome to the University prospective students, and we organise a number of events for that purpose, including open days. In addition, special arrangements can be made outside of those events for groups to come on campus at a time which is convenient for the visitors and for the University. A good deal of information for prospective students is available at *www.ucd.ie*. I enclose for your information a copy of the current Undergraduate Prospectus, and further inquiries can be directed to Ms Elish Carr, Deputy Admissions Officer.

However, it must be clearly understood that it would not be feasible for groups of visitors to "sit in at the back of random lectures asking difficult real life questions of the lecturers" as suggested in your letter. Naturally, such behaviour could have serious consequences for the safety and welfare of our students and staff. Therefore, you should not come on campus at any time with such intentions in mind. If any such incidents occur, the University will have no option but to take whatever steps are necessary to safeguard its students and staff.

Yours sincerely,

John Coman
Corporate and Legal Affairs Secretary

[Enclosed: 200-page Prospectus]

Also, one of the three Universities responded by sending the Gardaí to talk to Mr Bill Stevens at the University of Real Life. The Gardaí were unable to find Mr Stevens.

Oifig An Aire Oideachais agus Eolaíochta,
Sráid Maoilbhríde,
Baile Átha Cliath 1.

Telefón: 01-873 4700
Facs: 01-872 9093

Office of the Minister for Education and Science,
Marlborough Street
Dublin 1.

Telephone: 01-873 4700
Facs: 01-872 9093

Dear Mr Stevens,

The Minister for Education and Science, Mr. Noel
Dempsey T.D., has asked me to acknowledge your
recent letter regarding your proposed third level
institution. Enquiries are being made about this matter
and a further letter will issue as soon as possible.

Ronnie Ryan
Private Secretary

Oifig An Aire Oideachais agus Eolaíochta,
Sráid Maoilbhríde,
Baile Átha Cliath 1.

Telefón: 01-873 4700
Facs: 01-872 9093

Office of the Minister for Education and Science,
Marlborough Street
Dublin 1.

Telephone: 01-873 4700
Facs: 01-872 9093

Our Ref: 0403331/DG

8 September 2004

Dear Mr Stevens,

I refer to your recent letter regarding your proposed third level institution.

Unfortunately, no funding is currently available for the establishment of a new
third level facility.

The National Qualifications Authority of Ireland's main object is to establish
and maintain a framework of qualifications for the development, recognition
and award of qualifications in the State, based on standards of knowledge, skill
or competence to be acquired by learners. I would suggest that you contact the
NQAI on 01 887 1500 for further advice on this matter.

I am sorry I cannot be of
further assistance on
this matter.

Mr Noel Dempsey TD
Minister for Education and Science

Absurdly Yours
THE Michael Nugent LETTERS

PART THREE

DAFT DISPATCHES

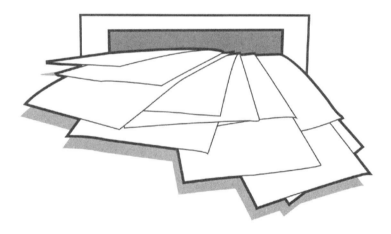

"...Unfortunately, as a cruise ship is in effect a floating hotel, it is inevitable that you will from time to time be able to see water..."

- Cunard Line responds to a potential cruise customer who is afraid of seeing water.

3 May 2004

Reservations Manager,
Restaurant Patrick Guilbaud,
Merrion Hotel

Dear Reservations Manager,

I wish to book a table at your restaurant later this month, but first I wish to fill you in on a somewhat delicate matter which I know you will treat with discretion.

Though we are not related, I look almost identical to Mr Liam Lawlor. This used to be a harmless diversion: a very small number of people would say "Ah, it's the man", or thank me for favours they imagined I had done for them. However, since the Tribunals started, Mr Lawlor's face and reputation have grown.

The doorman at my bank now greets me as 'Mr Big', and cashiers jokingly ask whether I want my money in a brown envelope. Last month outside the Clarence Hotel, a complete stranger threatened to throw me into the River Liffey. Sometimes people think I am Mr Ray Burke. We don't look alike; they just mix up the three of us.

I therefore wish to book a table shielded by a screen, with more screens, or perhaps potted palms or other tropical plants, creating a subtle passageway to and from the door, with your staff behaving as if this was normal, and making no snide remarks about prison food as has happened in another restaurant.

This is an important business meeting. Nothing must upset my colleague. This will be his first trip to Ireland, and he should be welcomed accordingly. He speaks no English, but is sensitive to tone of voice and visual cues. He looks not unlike Mr Tony Orlando of Dawn ('Tie a Yellow Ribbon Round the Old Oak Tree') and he is on the Atkins diet.

Yours sincerely,

Matthew Langford

Mr Matthew Langford

Reservations Manager,
Restaurant Patrick Guilbaud,
Merrion Hotel,
Upper Merrion Street,
Dublin 2, Ireland

RESTAURANT PATRICK GUILBAUD

7th May, 2004

Dear Mr. Langford,

We would be delighted to look after you and your guest later this month.

We have the perfect table for your requirements in the main restaurant, or perhaps you might like to use the Private Dining Room?

We are open for lunch and dinner Tuesday to Saturday, and you are welcome to come a little bit earlier than our normal opening times if you wish.

We can, of course, cater for your guest's dietary needs.

I look forward to hearing from you,

Yours sincerely,

Katherine Garnier

26 April 2004

Mr Uri Geller

Dear Uri,

I am writing to warn you of a great danger. You have been my guru ever since you started my late father's watch. I have read your books, wear your Double Crystal Necklace, and marvel at your charity work and miracles. Ever since your inspirational ParaScience Pack started me on the road to astral travel, I have devoted every Sunday to leaving my body.

Uri, on Easter Sunday, my astral journey took me to a hotel in London, where you told me to look at my watch. When I did, it had stopped at 12:13. Then a blinding flash of light returned me to my body. I was shivering and drenched in sweat, although my real watch was still working. Last Sunday and this Sunday, I have been unable to leave my body. Then I told a friend from London, and she said you had been appearing at the Hilton Hotel on Easter Sunday.

When we realised that Easter Sunday was April 11th, we recalled your recent warnings about the number 11. We did some calculations, and this is what we found. 'April Eleven' has 11 letters, as well as being the 11th day of the month. 'Hilton Hotel' also has 11 letters, as has its parent company 'Hilton Group'. The hotel itself is located at 22 (=2 x 11) Park Lane, and its phone number is 020 7493 8000, the digits of which add up to 33 (=3 x 11). My watch stopped at 12:13. This is part of the sequence of 11:12:13, and is very nearly 44,000 (=4,000 x 11) seconds into the day.

This is all surely a sign of great danger. Did everything go okay at the Hilton? Can you describe the room in which you were appearing? Do you think that I should try to go there again on an astral journey? Or, as I don't seem able to leave my body right now, should I visit the Hilton in real life, and see if that reveals the message I have been given? Please let me know what to do.

Yours sincerely,

Connie Sheldon

Mrs Connie Sheldon

Mr Uri Geller,
Sonning, Berkshire,
RG4 6UR,
England

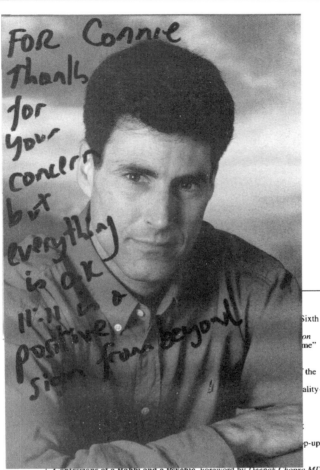

FOR Connie
Thanks
for
your
concern
but
everything
is ok
11:11 is a
positive
sign from beyond

Confessions of a Rabbi and a Psychic, Foreword by *Deepak Chopra MD*
with an Acknowledgement from His Holiness The Pope
Uri's Biography, **Uri Geller Magician or mystic?** by Jonathan Margolis
(Time Magazine European Correspondent) - "A fascinating, unjaded,
open-minded account of a great modern puzzle" - *Mail on Sunday*.
All these books are available on **www.amazon.com**
www.barnesandnoble.com www.amazon.co.uk or in major book shops.
Uri's inspirational set of five CDs- encompassing healing, meditation,
positivity and lots more-could help you immensely. Available to order on
his web site.
Please visit Uri's web site **www.urigeller.com**
E-mail Uri at **urigeller@compuserve.com**

Connie
get on my
web site
& see my
11:11 page
love
Uri

Front of card reads:
"For Connie. Thanks for
your concern, but
everything is ok. 11:11
is a positive sign from
beyond." Back of card
reads: "Connie, get on
my web site & see my
11:11 page. Love, Uri."

105

21 June 2004

Neil A Armstrong,
Lebanon, USA

Dear Professor Armstrong,

    I am writing a popular culture book that makes reference to your historic achievement in becoming the first man to walk on the moon. I would appreciate if you could confirm the accuracy of the following paragraphs that I intend to use.

    "The young Armstrong, a clean-cut all-American hero, bore an uncanny resemblance to the 1970s icon Ritchie Cunningham, as played by Ron Howard in 'Happy Days'. While the deeply envious Howard went on to direct 'Apollo 13', he would never emulate Armstrong's coolness, as a Gemini-8-space-docking, Apollo-11-moon-walking professor of aerospace engineering. Here's one example.

    "While walking on the moon, Armstrong enigmatically said: 'Good luck, Mr Gorsky!' He only explained this after Mr Gorsky died in 1995. As a child in Ohio, he had once climbed into a neighbour's garden to retrieve a baseball. The ball was below the bedroom window, and the young Armstrong overheard Mrs Gorsky shout at her husband: 'Oral sex? Oral sex you want? You'll get it when the kid next door walks on the moon!'

    "More recently, Armstrong has retired as Chairman of the Board of AIL Systems, and Howard appeared in the Andy Griffith Show Reunion 'Back to Mayberry'. Henry Winkler, who played Howard's 'Happy Days' co-star 'Fonzie', went on to direct 'Sabrina the Teenage Witch' and played the voice of Norville in 'Clifford's Puppy Days'."

Yours sincerely,

Jean Jackson

Jean Jackson

Neil A Armstrong,
P.O. Box 436,
Lebanon, OH 45036,
USA

NEIL A. ARMSTRONG
P.O. BOX 436
LEBANON, OH 45036

July 1 2004

Dear Ms. Jackson:

I am responding on behalf of Mr. Armstrong to your letter of 21 June.

The first paragraph appears to be someone's opinion, so it is impossible to confirm the accuracy of it.

The second paragraph is entirely false. I have been informed that it originated from a "comedy" skit performed by Buddy Hacket several years ago.

It is true that Mr. Armstrong retired from the EDO Corporation, which was formerly AIL Systems. I cannot confirm or deny the balance of that third paragraph.

I hope that this information is helpful to you. We appreciate the courtesy of your enquiry.

Sincerely,

Vivian White
Administrative Aide

26 July 2004

Mr John Leech,
Chief Executive,
Irish Water Safety,
Galway

Dear Mr Leech,

   I will be seventy next month, and I have always admired the daredevils who plunge over Niagara Falls in a barrel.

   On my birthday I plan to emulate their feat, but due to my condition I plan to go over a canal lock instead of a waterfall.

   This will be a very special event for me.

   I will pad the inside of the barrel with thick eiderdown and cushions, paint 'Happy 70th Birthday' on the outside, and have seventy lit candles on the top. Afterwards, we will have a celebratory family picnic.

   Can you please tell me, where is the highest canal lock in Ireland, with sufficient depth of water underneath for such an activity?

   Also, can you please give me a few expert words to counter the mild paranoia being expressed by some of my family?

   Yours sincerely,

   Annie Kirk

   Mrs Annie Kirk

Mr John Leech,
Chief Executive,
Irish Water Safety,
The Long Walk,
Galway

Irish Water Safety
Cumann Sábháilteacht Uisce

The Long Walk, Galway, Ireland.
An Bóthar Fada, Gaillimh, Éire.
Tel: 091 - 56 44 00   LoCall: 1890 420 202
Fax: 091 - 56 47 00   Email: info@iws.ie
Website: www.iws.ie

5th August 2004

Dear Mrs Kirk,

Thank you very much for your letter dated 26th July 2004 in relation to your 70th birthday, and may I take this opportunity to wish you a very happy birthday.

The highest fall on a river lock in Ireland is the Ardnacrusha Lock on the River Shannon, which is operated by the ESB. The highest fall from a Canal Lock near Dublin would be the 13th Lock on the Grand Canal west of Hazelhatch. Or indeed the Westmoreland Lock, where the Grand Canal enters the river Liffey at the end of Sir John Rogerson's Quay, both of which are operated by Waterways Ireland.

In any event, I would recommend that you celebrate your birthday with your family in a more positive way that will give good leadership and example to your family and others. For instance, you could do an open water swim on river, lake or at sea. Perhaps you could do it for your favourite charity; our Association is always seeking funds and we would be happy to receive any donation.

Before you decide on what activity that you would like to complete to celebrate your birthday, I recommend that you be passed fit by your own family doctor. Whatever activity that you decide, I wish you a safe and enjoyable day and many more years of good health.

Yours in safety,

Lt Cdr John F M Leech
Chief Executive

The Irish Water Safety Association is the statutory body established to promote water safety in Ireland.   Tá Cumann Sábháilteacht Uisce ina bhord reachtúil a bunaíodh le sábháilteacht uisce a chothú in Éireann.

25 April 2004

Congregation for the Causes of Saints,
Vatican City, Rome, Italy

Dear Cardinal Martins,

     I wish to propose a new type of Saint. Sadly, we live in a world of celebrity-inspired belief systems; Madonna endorses Kabbalah, John Travolta Scientology and Jennifer Aniston the secular Atkins Diet. In this swirl of confused messages, the Church could influence wavering minds by canonizing the following as the first twelve 'Celebrity Apostles':

- Saint Mel Gibson, whose movie 'The Passion of the Christ' has reminded the world that God will show mercy to those who love Him, and visit the iniquity of the fathers upon the children of those who hate Him.

- Saint Daniel O'Donnell, the clean-cut Irish singer who has raised over £1 million for Romanian orphans. He still invites fans into his house for nothing more sordid than a cup of tea.

- Saint Susan Sarandon, 'the Prodigal Saint': despite appearing in the feminist gore-fest 'Thelma and Louise', she now campaigns against domestic violence and for gun control.

- Saint Jimmy Saville, who provided in 'Jim'll Fix It' a miracle factory for spiritually malnourished children. He now runs marathons for charity while in his eighties.

- Saint Britney Spears, who made virginity 'cool' by singing erotic songs while publicly saving herself for marriage. This subtle incongruity cleverly decoupled desire and consummation.

- Saint Bob Geldof, who has not only brought world peace and multinational fiscal reform closer, but also has brought the Protestant Bono to meet the Holy Father in the Vatican.

- Saint Dan Aykroyd, whose portrayal of Elwood Blues saving the Chicago orphanage is etched in the souls of a generation. He also popularised the phrase 'We're on a mission from God'.

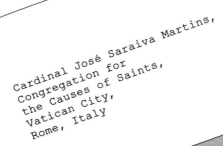

Cardinal José Saraiva Martins,
Congregation for
the Causes of Saints,
Vatican City,
Rome, Italy

- Saint Suzanne Summers, whose exercise regime brings self-esteem to the faithful. The Inflatable Flex-a-Ball is to the temples of our bodies what prayer is to the souls within.

- Saint Niall Quinn, the Irish footballer who has donated over £1 million to children's hospitals. He also came to the fore as a peacemaker during Ireland's World Cup crisis in Saipan.

- Saint Tommy Hilfiger, whose 'trendy' fashions adorn the bodies of the 'hip'. His canonization would reach out to young Catholics who want to look 'preppy with an urban edge'.

- Saint Bill O'Reilly, whose fearless campaign for traditional Christian values has dominated Fox News. Saint Mel Gibson has already bought the screen rights to his novel 'Those Who Trespass'.
- Saint Lisa Tarbuck, whose father Jimmy was a cheeky but clean Liverpudlian comic. Having followed in her father's footsteps, her fame has eclipsed even his among today's young Catholics.

   With a 'hip' slogan ("We're Catholic, we're 'with it' – are you with us?") these twelve 'Celebrity Apostles' would counter such communistic Catholic icons as Fidel Castro, Michael Moore and Liam Gallagher of Oasis. They would also provide a sanctimonious contrast to the heathen celebrities who 'trash' hotel rooms and engage in bizarre sexual deviancies.

   Yours sincerely,

   Patricia Holmes

   Mrs Patricia Holmes

CONGREGAZIONE
DELLE CAUSE DEI SANTI
———

Rome, 13 May 2004

Ms. Holmes,

   This Congregation for the Causes of Saints acknowledges receipt of your letter of 25th April last.

10 August 2004

Mr Michael Buckley,
Group Chief Executive,
AIB plc

Dear Mr Buckley,

I write regarding the media slur that AIB overcharged your customers for ten years. As you and I know, the reality is that you simply forgot "in an administrative sense" to inform the regulators that you were overcharging customers; but of course this nuance is beyond the financial nous of the media hyenas.

Sadly, the world is changing. Once, you could set up offshore management bonus schemes with no 'tax issues'. Then suddenly you had to pay all the DIRT tax on those culture-of-the-time non-resident accounts. And now... THIS!

It is clear why you looked so sad during the recent press conferences. When enduring similar ordeals, I find it useful to defuse the tension with a joke. Here is a bank-related one you might consider:

> Paddy Mac is a bank teller. A frog asks him
> for a loan. His only collateral is an old
> ornament, and the fact that his father is
> Mick Jagger. Paddy Mac asks his manager what
> he thinks the ornament is worth. And the
> manager says: "It's a knick-knack, Paddy Mac,
> give the frog a loan, his old man's a Rolling
> Stone."

Anyway, as a gesture of solidarity, I would like to transfer some funds from their current merchant bank to your good selves. What is the most tax-efficient vehicle? As you're probably watching the cash flow, I enclose €10 towards the administrative costs of dealing with this query.

Yours sincerely,

George Wilson

Mr George Wilson

Mr Michael Buckley,
Group Chief Executive,
AIB plc, Bank Centre,
Ballsbridge,
Dublin 4

AIB Group
Office of the
Group Chief Executive

Bankcentre
Ballsbridge
Dublin 4
Ireland

Telephone +353 1 6600 311
Facsimile +353 1 6603 063
www.aib.ie

17th September 2004.

Dear Mr. Wilson,

Thank you for your letter of the 10th September addressed to Mr. Michael Buckley.

With regard to responding to your previous letter of the 10th August 2004, we did in fact attempt on two occasions to hand deliver a response but unfortunately, we were advised that you were not known at the address.

We wished to hand deliver the letter as we were returning the €10 you had kindly sent us.

On the basis that we may have somehow called to the wrong address or been misinformed that you were not known there, we are writing on this occasion by post in the hope that you will receive the letter and might contact us to provide clarification regarding your address.

It would also help if you could provide a contact telephone number so that we can contact you if we encounter further difficulties in locating you.

We look forward to hearing from you.

Yours sincerely,

Denise FitzGibbon

Denise FitzGibbon,
PA to Mr. Michael Buckley

26 July 2004

Cunard Line,
Southampton,
United Kingdom

Dear Cunard,

    I have just won a considerable sum on the lottery, and I have always promised myself that I would take a luxury cruise if I won. This has been my dream, and now it can come true.

    However, I have a medical condition called hydrophobia, which makes me afraid of water. I do NOT have rabies, which is also called hydrophobia. But I am absolutely terrified of water. Even thinking about the sea makes me anxious, nauseous and irritable.

    Is it possible to arrange a cruise where all of the ship's facilities (casinos, sundecks etc) can be reached and used without seeing any water, and where a crew member can assist me on and off the ship so that I do not see any water?

    Yours sincerely,

    Ger Matthews

    Mr Ger Matthews

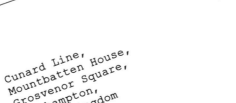

Cunard Line,
Mountbatten House,
Grosvenor Square,
Southampton,
United Kingdom

CUNARD

THE MOST FAMOUS OCEAN LINERS IN THE WORLD ™

21 August 2004

Dear Mr Matthews,

Thank you for your letter of 26 July and your interest in booking a Cunard holiday. Firstly, may I congratulate you on your lottery win.

Unfortunately, as a cruise ship is in effect a floating hotel it is inevitable that you will from time to time be able to see water, especially when utilising the facilities such as the open decks. You can of course minimise this by taking action such as booking an inside cabin, requesting a table in the centre of the restaurant and avoiding promenade and the open decks.

It would also greatly depend on the cruise you choose, as some cruises include a number of tender ports. (The ship anchors from the shore and passengers are transferred to shore in a small craft, known as a tender.) It is also highly likely that you will be able to see water when leaving and entering the ship at other ports. Whilst not wishing to deter you, the above preventative measures may avoid viewing the sea, but you should keep in mind that you would be on a moving vessel and the ocean motion would still be felt.

May I suggest that, if you are still considering a cruise, P&O Cruises arrange day trip visits in Southampton. The day consists of a tour of one of our ships and lunch on board. There is a £25 charge for this. If you would like further information please do not hesitate to contact me.

I do hope we may have the pleasure of welcoming you on board in the future.

Yours sincerely,

Tina Sanderson
Senior Passenger Relations Executive

CUNARD LINE Richmond House, Terminus Terrace, Southampton, SO14 3PN
Switchboard Telephone (Within UK) 0845 3 585 585 (Outside UK) +44 (0)23 8065 5085 Facsimile +44 (0)23 8022 7920 Web www.cunard.co.uk
Cunard Line is a business name of Cunard Seabourn Ltd, a company incorporated in England under registration number 3553628
Registered Office: 5 Gainsford Street, London, SE1 2NE, United Kingdom

10 September 2004

Ambassador Extraordinary
and Plenipotentiary of
the People's Republic of China

Your Excellency,

       The Irish Taoiseach, Mr Bertie Ahern, has asked citizens
to consider business opportunities in Asia.

       My initial research has revealed that your Government is
upgrading schoolbooks to remove the claim that the Great Wall
can be seen from space, after Yang Liwei did not see it on his
recent orbit. I have an alternative proposal that would
attract tourists to China, while keeping intact the Wall's
place in space history.

       Here's my line of thinking: Apollo 17 commander Gene
Cernan said he saw the Wall from space. Why would this icon of
American capitalism falsely promote a communist Wall? Perhaps
the Wall is just hard to see from space because the colours of
its materials blend into the landscape?

       If so, I suggest clearing away the sand from the Wall,
then painting it with very bright luminous paint. And I would
like to tender for this job. I believe the Wall is 6,700 km
long by between 5 and 10 metres wide and between 5 and 15
metres high. That would give a surface area of between 91
million and 271 million square metres, with probably a bit
more for the guard towers, which I would have to see before
giving an accurate quote.

       We have painted almost two hundred houses and a very
large warehouse in Tallaght Industrial Estate. But this would
be our biggest job yet, so I propose that we only paint part
of the Wall, as part of a larger team that you would put
together in China. I look forward to a positive reply.

       Yours sincerely,

       Maxwell Waters

       Mr Maxwell Waters

His Excellency Mr Sha Hailin,
Ambassador Extraordinary
and Plenipotentiary of
the People's Republic of China

中 华 人 民 共 和 国 驻 爱 尔 兰 大 使 馆
EMBASSY OF THE PEOPLE'S REPUBLIC OF CHINA

40 Ailesbury Road
Dublin 4, Ireland

Tel: 00353-1-2691707
Fax: 00353-1-2839938

September 16th, 2004

Dear Mr. Maxwell Waters,

We received your letter to our Ambassador. Thank you very much for your concern about China.

The Great Wall is now the historical heritage of China as well as the world. We have always been attaching great importance to preserve it.

We are not sure if your suggestion could be followed but we will pass it on to the relevant Department in China.

Again, thanks for your letter.

With kind regards,

Yours sincerely,

Tony Wang
Chinese Embassy

21 September 2004

Mr Owen Keegan,
Director of Traffic, Dublin City

Dear Mr Keegan,

I have an idea to help traffic in Dublin, boost the development of Irish football, and commemorate the giants of the game. I would welcome any advice or support.

Elderly football pundits such as John Giles, Eamon Dunphy and Liam Brady have identified a reason for the decline in natural football skills: as children, they played football on the streets morning, noon and night. Plastic ball or tennis ball, captains pick sides, jumpers or lampposts for goalposts.

We could easily recreate those days, by allotting specific streets to children's football. Choose streets that don't hinder bus routes, but that do inconvenience drivers of private cars. Use lampposts as floodlights, and have a fund to compensate residents and shopkeepers for the inevitable broken windows.

To promote the idea, we could commemorate the giants of Irish football by making twelve-foot statues of them playing football. These giant statues would be located in the middle of the streets, as mini-roundabouts to slow down traffic. As a bonus, tourists would flock to Europe's new football capital.

Imagine driving around Dublin, circling giant statues of Eamon Dunphy on Drumcondra Road, John Giles near the Four Courts, Liam Brady in Whitehall, Dave O'Leary in Glasnevin, Robbie Keane in Tallaght, Damien Duff in Rathfarnham. Jack Charlton could be fishing off O'Connell Bridge, and a special conciliatory statue by the GPO would display Mick McCarthy and Roy Keane shaking hands.

What do you think? I plan to approach some major companies to seek sponsorship.

Yours sincerely,

Eddie O'Carroll

Mr Eddie O'Carroll

Mr Owen Keegan,
Director of Traffic,
Block 2, Floor 4,
Fishamble Street,
Dublin 8

Dublin City Council
Comhairle Cathrach Bhaile Átha Cliath

Owen P. Keegan, Director of Traffic & Assistant City Manager,
Civic Offices, Wood Quay, Dublin 8

Oifigí na Cathrach, An Ché Adhmaid, Baile Átha Cliath
T. 01 672 2837 F. 01 672 2221 E. owen.keegan@dublincity.ie

23rd September 2004

Dear Mr O'Carroll,

I acknowledge receipt of your letter of 21st September regarding the allotting of specific streets in the city to children's football.

I regret to inform you that the City Council is not in a position to support such a proposal due to the inconvenience and safety risks that it is likely to generate for the general public.

It is not the policy of the City Council to actively seek to 'inconvenience' car drivers but, instead, to make alternatives to the car more attractive.

We regret that changes such as those you suggest are likely to create increased congestion and problems of access for all road users in the city.

In this light, the City Council would be totally opposed to such actions.

Yours sincerely,

Owen P. Keegan
**Director of Traffic &
Assistant City Manager**

Head Office, Civic Offices, Wood Quay, Dublin 8, Ireland
Oifigí na Cathrach, An Ché Adhmaid, B.Á.C. 8, Éire
T. 01 672 2222 **www.dublincity.ie**

9 July 2004

The Secretary,
International Federation of
the Phonographic Industry,
Zurich,
Switzerland

Dear Secretary,

I am a teenage girl living in Dublin, Ireland, and my friends all tell me I would make a great Page Three model. However, I love my family very much, and they would die of shame if they saw my picture in the paper.

Can you please send me a list of newspapers that are <u>NOT</u> sold in Ireland, and that will print tasteful topless pictures? I will <u>NOT</u> do any fully nude shots, or in fact anything below the waist, as my bum is too big.

Thank you very much for your help.

I am very shy.

Yours sincerely,

Noelle O'Brien

Noelle O'Brien

International Federation of
the Phonographic Industry,
Utoquai 37, Postfach 581,
CH-8024 Zurich,
Switzerland

International Federation of the Phonographic Industry

Utoquai 37 - Postfach 581 - 8024 Zurich - Switzerland

July 22, 2004

DW/mb

Dear Ms O'Brien,

I thank you for your kind letter dated July 9, 2004.

Unfortunately, being the Secretary of the International Federation of the **Phono**graphic Industry, I am afraid I cannot be of any assistance.

With kind regards,

Dr. Daniel Wehrli

24 April 2004

Mr Brian McConnell,
Chief Executive, Permanent TSB

Dear Mr McConnell,

My family has deposited with the Irish Permanent since before I was born, so it is with sadness that I complain about your recent radio advert. It is sad as you run a good bank, with good officers and staff, and this lapse is very much out of character.

Your advert starts with a song – 'Free Permanent TSB' – that parodies the 1980s protest anthem 'Free Nelson Mandela'. This not only trivialises the sacrifice of former President Mandela and the music of the Specials, but your gratuitous use of faked Jamaican accents slanderously links a warm and friendly Caribbean nation with the horrors of the South African apartheid regime.

This could not be further from the truth. Jamaica is a cultural cornucopia pulsating to the rhythmic beat of genuine reggae. Just contrast any Bob Marley record from 'Natty Dread' to 'Uprising' with your reprise of the puerile accents adopted by 10CC in 'Dreadlock Holiday'. Your advert may not have explicitly sung of being mugged in Jamaica by "four faces, one masked, a brother from the gutter", but morally you might as well have. Shame on you.

Jamaica may only be a mere blip on your fiscal radar screens, but that does not excuse this gratuitous slur on its entirely democratic political system. We would rightly be insulted if the Bank of Jamaica advertised its services with a Daniel O'Donnell mimic singing a parody of the anti-Nazi anthem 'Spring-time for Hitler and Germany'. Surely we should have the courtesy to avoid visiting a similar smear upon the Jamaicans.

Yours sincerely,

Geraldine Costello

Mrs Geraldine Costello

Mr Brian McConnell,
Chief Executive, Permanent TSB,
Irish Life Centre,
Lower Abbey Street,
Dublin 1

56-59 St. Stephen's Green,
Dublin 2

Telephone 01 661 5577
Facsimile 01 661 5828
www.permanenttsb.ie

4th May 2004

Dear Mrs Costello,

Thank you for your letter in which you outline your concerns over our use of the 'Free **permanent tsb**' song to promote our range of products.

I am glad to allay your concerns with the news that we will not be using this particular melody in the future.

Yours sincerely,

Brian McConnell
Chief Executive

permanent tsb is a trading name of Irish Life & Permanent. Irish Life & Permanent plc is regulated by the Central Bank of Ireland
Directors: Roy Douglas (chairman), David Went (Group Chief Executive), Gillian Bowler (UK), Denis Casey, Peter Fitzpatrick, Monty Hikowitz (South Africa),
Richard Hooper, Patrick Kenny, Brian McConnell, Kieran McGowan, Kevin Murphy, Patrick O'Neill, Muriel Scorer, Barry SHeehan
Registered office: Irish Life Centre, Lower Abbey Street, Dublin 1, Ireland. Registered in Dublin. Registered No 222332. A tied Insurance Agent for Irish Life Assurance plc

3 May 2004

The Honorable Tommy G Thompson,
Secretary of Health and Human Services,
Washington, USA

Dear Secretary Thompson,

My wife and I plan to return to Wisconsin, where we can once again watch the Brewers, visit the Baraboo Circus World and become active in the Republican Party! Anyway, here is an idea to improve both the health service and the economy.

Two years ago I developed a mole on my face which rendered me open to gentle 'ribbing' from workmates. Then my wife, who spends her Saturdays rummaging in second-hand charity shops, found an elaborately illustrated Victorian medical book that showed how to 'strangle' such moles by simply tying string around them. This we did, but using dental floss, repeating the procedure every few days with ever-tighter knots, more secure than the cuffs at the Houdini Historical Center in Appleton. Today I still have in a jar by my bed the small, black, hard, shrivelled corpse of my mole.

This made us think: why do we ask doctors to do what we can do ourselves? It wastes our money and the doctor's time, which should be kept free for 'serious' medical procedures. We have since removed several verrucas with vinegar-soaked sandpaper, and re-sculpted an ingrown toenail using tweezers and a Stanley knife blade. And we will soon be using the dental floss 'strangle' method to remove my increasingly uncomfortable haemorrhoids.

Think of the savings that could be made if you were to encourage responsible use of 'home surgery'. Clearly not for internal operations, but for basic procedures that require no more than a good eye and a steady hand. You could produce a 'how-to' booklet, with details on where to buy medical equipment. What do you think? I look forward to meeting you when we return to Wisconsin and become active in the Party.

Yours sincerely,

Charles Johnson

Mr Charles Johnson

The Hon Tommy G Thompson,
Secretary of Health
and Human Services,
200 Independence Avenue SW,
Washington, DC 20201, USA

NIAMS

National Institutes of Health

**National Institute of
Arthritis and
Musculoskeletal and
Skin Diseases**

US DEPARTMENT OF HEALTH
AND HUMANS ERVICES
Public Health Service
Bethesda, MD 20892-2350

Dear Mr. Johnson:

Secretary Thompson has asked me to thank you for your recent letter, and to respond directly to you. I am the director of the National Institute of Arthritis and Musculoskeletal and Skin Diseases (NIAMS), a part of the U.S. Department of Health and Human Services' National Institutes of Health. NIAMS is a major Federal organization supporting research on skin diseases and disorders.

We appreciate hearing from people who have ideas about alternative treatments. The procedures that you describe are well known in folk medicine. While usually effective, there are some concerns. The manipulations must be done in a clean if not sterile setting. Otherwise there is the potential for local and occasionally more severe skin infection. But probably more important is that the nature of the skin growth must be ascertained.

While such a "mole" will usually be a benign growth, there is the small but real chance that it is skin cancer. If that is not recognized at or prior to the removal, the opportunity for complete removal may be lost and with it the ability to prevent later, sometimes severe or even fatal, consequences. Also, some benign growths may bleed severely, even uncontrollably, when manipulated in this way. We cannot recommend such home surgeries when the nature of the skin growth is not known in advance. That typically requires the involvement of an appropriately trained health professional, such as a dermatologist (skin doctor). These removals are usually so simple that the removal can often be done at the same visit at which the nature of the growth is determined.

We welcome your suggestions, and assure you they have been considered. In this case, for the reasons cited above, we cannot recommend such alternatives. Thank you for sharing your thoughts about the possible advantages of home surgery.

Sincerely,

Stephen I. Katz, M.D., Ph.D.
Director
National Institute of Arthritis and
 Musculoskeletal and Skin Diseases

9 July 2004

Reservations Manager,
Dromoland Castle

Dear Reservations Manager,

My wife and I are from Texas, and I would like details on staying in your hotel between August 30th and Sept 2nd. These are the dates of the Republican Convention in New York when President Bush will be nominated for re-election – and his acceptance speech will coincide with our twentieth wedding anniversary!

We would like to book the room in which President Bush slept during his recent visit. I will arrive a day early and decorate the room with American flags and Republican Party memorabilia. I will also bring a small podium from behind which I will introduce the Convention speakers to my wife as they appear on television.

While in our room, I will wear a Superman outfit and a Spiro Agnew campaign badge, and my wife will dress as Andy Warhol for 15 minutes per day, and the Bionic Woman thereafter. Each day, we will order broccoli for our room, but we will not eat it (we will of course pay). ONLY your room-service staff should know about this.

We will dress formally elsewhere in the castle, in the style of characters from the television series Dallas. The ONLY time we will appear in costume outside of our room will be for a BRIEF photo, using the podium, in the garden where President Bush held his press conference. We will dress formally to and from the garden.

Can you oblige? This is a very special weekend for us.

Yours sincerely,

Thomas Lucy

Mr Thomas Lucy

Reservations Manager,
Dromoland Castle,
Newmarket-on-Fergus,
County Clare

Dromoland Castle

Newmarket-on-Fergus, Co. Clare, Ireland.
Tel: 061-368144   E-mail: sales@dromoland.ie
Fax: 061-363355   Web-Site: www.dromoland.ie

16/07/2004

Dear Mr. Lucy,

I am sorry to advise you that our Presidential Suite is fully booked for a period of ten days over the dates you have requested.

Unfortunately, we regret that we are unable to offer the accommodation to you at this time.

We wish you and your wife a wonderful anniversary, and the best of luck in your search for a suitable venue for your celebrations.

I remain yours,

Bláthnaid Sexton
Reservations Manager

Dromoland Castle Holdings Ltd.

Directors: Gavin K. O'Reilly (Chairman)
Mark Nolan (Managing)
James P. Moriarty (US)
John O'Brien (US)
Patrick J. Rooney (US)
Edward L. Barlow (US)
Malcolm G. Chace, Jnr. (US)
J. Kevin Gilgan (US)

USA: Marketing Office:

P.O. Box 28966, Atlanta, Georgia, 30358-0966,
Tel: 770-612-1701. Fax: 770-612-1725.
Toll Free: 1-800-346-7007
Place of Registration: Ireland

Registered Office:
11 South Mall, Cork, Ireland.
Registration No.: 120693

20 September 2004

Mr Brian Goggin,
Group Chief Executive Officer,
Bank of Ireland

Dear Mr Goggin,

As a university student I am impressed by your bank's modern approach to sexuality. I am writing in response to your television advert ("I hope they're not up...") in which you offer financial assistance to couples who need somewhere to have sex when they come home late and their parents are still up.

My girlfriend Maria and I have the same problem. Last weekend, for the first time ever, we managed to reach my bedroom unheard, and Maria slipped home unnoticed after a night of passion. Unfortunately, my mother was tidying my bedroom the next day and found Maria's delicates draped over a chair. I pretended that they were mine, and put them on to convince her.

Frankly, everybody involved is now extremely uncomfortable at even the thought of any future sexual activity in that room. So Maria and I would like to take you up on the offer in your advert. We want to jointly take out a bank loan sufficient to hire a hotel room one night a week for the foreseeable future. Could you please send me whatever forms we need to complete?

I enclose €10 to cover the administrative costs of replying to this request.

Yours sincerely,

John Murray

John Murray

Mr Brian Goggin,
Group Chief Executive Officer,
Bank of Ireland,
Lower Baggot Street,
Dublin 2

Bank of Ireland ⬮

Customer Care Unit
Head Office
Lower Baggot Street, Dublin 2
Tel 1850 753 357
Fax +353 (0)1 662 0853
email careline@boimail.com
www.bankofireland.ie

8th October 2004

Dear Mr. Murray,

Thank you for your recent letter.

Although this is the first loan request of this type that we've encountered, as our brochure says: 'lending money is our business, how you spend it is yours.'

So please feel free to contact your local branch in Westland Row and our staff will be happy to discuss your financial requirements and assist you in whatever way they can.

There is no charge for this service, so I'm returning your €10.

Kind regards,

Bernie O'Donnell
Customer Careline Manager

24 April 2004

His Majesty,
King Gyanendra Bir Bikram Shah Dev,
Kathmandu, Nepal

Your Majesty,

The Irish Taoiseach, Mr Bertie Ahern, has asked citizens to consider business opportunities in Asia. My initial research shows that Nepal could be the tourism hub of the East, boasting both the top of the world and a country that would be among the world's largest if all of the mountains were flattened out.

Your Majesty, have you ever thought of building a secure scaffolding route on Mount Everest? If so, I would like to tender for this exciting job. Think supported scaffolds (hod-carrier on a building site) at the early stages, and suspended scaffolds (window-cleaner on a skyscraper) nearer the summit.

Tourism would soar, as Everest would be both the planet's highest peak, and highest scaffold-assisted peak. And to the usual categories of 'first' ascents, we could add a new record for the most safety-conscious ascent.

I have already scaffolded almost a hundred building sites and a multi-purpose activity centre with a 'modern' design incorporating mountain-style overhangs. But this would be my biggest job yet, so I propose that I work as part of a larger team that you would put together in Nepal. I look forward to a positive reply.

Yours sincerely,

John Stephens

Mr John Stephens

His Majesty
King Gyanendra Bir Bikram Shah Dev,
Narayanhity Royal Palace,
Kathmandu, Nepal

His Majesty's Government

MINISTRY OF CULTURE, TOURISM & CIVIL AVIATION

Tourism Industry Division

Fax: 00977-1-227281
Phone: 247037, 256228,
            247580, 256234,
            256231, 247041
E-mail: tourism@mail.com.np

Tourist Service Centre Building
Bhrikuti Mandap. Kathmandu. Nepal.

Ref. No. 44

July 20, 2004

Dear Mr. Stephens,

I have the honor to refer to your letter dated 24 April 2004 regarding the proposal of building a secure scaffolding route on Mount Sagarmatha.

As per the decision of this Ministry, I would like to inform you that His Majesty's Government does not feel appropriate to build such kind of scaffolding on the climbing route of prestigious world's highest peak, Mount Sagarmatha.

Thank you very much for your keen interest to promote our mountain tourism.

Sincerely yours,

P.B. Tandukar
Under Secretary

3 May 2004

Head of Exhibitions,
Australian Museum,
Sydney

Dear Head of Exhibitions,

I am a travelling performance artist, and I would like to suggest an exhibition for your museum. It is inspired by your 'Death: The Last Taboo' exhibition last year, and the British Museum of Science's ambitious plan to exhibit a decomposing human body.

I understand that the British project is endangered by practical and ethical concerns raised by pathologists and bereavement counsellors. My alternative project would remove these complications, while maintaining, and even adding to, the artistic integrity of the original concept.

I have provisionally entitled it: 'He Gave His Right Arm: the Decomposition Comparison'.

I plan to have my right arm surgically amputated and displayed in a vacuum-filled glass case. Then I will undergo a strenuous programme of weight-training to build up my left arm. Every day, I will have my developing left arm photographed beside the exhibit of my decomposing right arm. This will facilitate an ongoing comparison between growth and decay, as well as life and death itself.

Would you be interested in hosting this exhibition? I do not need sponsorship, as I have sufficient funds to travel and maintain myself. I am doing this purely for its artistic worth. I should add that I am left-handed, so this would not hinder my ongoing artistic output.

Yours sincerely,

Ernie Ferguson

Mr Ernie Ferguson

Head of Exhibitions,
Australian Museum,
6 College Street,
Sydney

PUBLIC PROGRAMS
Ph: (02) 9320 6146   Fax: (02) 9320 6069
Internet: lainad@austmus.gov.au

AUSTRALIAN MUSEUM

6 College Street
Sydney NSW 2010
Phone (02) 9320 6000
www.amonline.net.au
ABN 85 407 224 698

24th June 2004

Dear Mr. Ferguson,

Thank you for your letter of 3rd May and your interest in our institution and exhibition program.

'Death: the Last Taboo' is an exhibition that has attracted much attention and a great deal of acclaim in respect of the way it approached a sensitive subject. We are glad that you also found it of interest.

Your proposal is challenging, but we must decline the opportunity you offer.

The Australian Museum is an institution with defined mission and objectives, and this medium of performance art does not fall within our exhibition criteria.

Thank you, however, for considering the Australian Museum.

Yours sincerely,

Laina De Winne

11 July 2004

Mr Seán Kelly, President,
Gaelic Athletic Association

A chara,

　　This weekend's matches showed why Gaelic games are the most exciting in the world.

　　First we had the exhilarating mêlée after Tipp's Benny Dunne pulled across Jerry O'Connor's legs, and the heated exchanges as Cork's keeper Donal Óg Cusack was being treated for his head injury. Then we had the usual altercations that typify any clash between Limerick and Kerry, with more to enjoy in the replay.

　　So here is my idea. I have a tooth that I found on the Páirc Na nGael pitch after this year's Munster hurling semi-final. Based on where I found it, I suspect that it used to belong to Limerick captain TJ Ryan or Cork's Jonathan O'Callaghan. I assume that it was dislodged during their exciting clash early in the game.

　　When I got home, I put it in a jewellery case which I borrowed from the wife, and labelled it: 'REAL MEN PLAY GAA'. I now carry it everywhere with great pride. I regularly take it out when televised soccer games show sissy millionaires rolling in agony when tripped up by other sissy millionaires.

　　Then, watching this weekend's games, it dawned on me that there must be loads of similar memorabilia around the country. So I plan to gather it all together, and donate it to the GAA museum at Croke Park for a 'REAL MEN PLAY GAA' display.

　　I can collect match reports, photographs, bandages, medical records etc. In fact, any memorabilia of REAL MEN, playing on normally despite physical injury, will perfectly capture the spirit I am trying to convey. Would the GAA Museum be interested in this display?

　　Is mise le meas,

Jimmy Roche

Mr Jimmy Roche

Mr Seán Kelly,
President,
Gaelic Athletic Association,
Croke Park Stadium,
Dublin 3

Cumann Lúthchleas Gael

ÁRD STIÚRTHÓIR: LIAM Ó MAOLMHICHÍL

Cumann Lúthchleas Gael,
Páirc an Chrócaigh,
Baile Átha Cliath 3.
Guthán: 01-8363222 Fax: 01-8366420

6 August 2004

Dear Mr Roche,

The President has asked me to refer to your letter in regard to your "collection".

He has said that, even though he is a Kerryman, he can detect a "wind up" from a thousand yards.

Yours sincerely,

Danny Lynch
PRO

3 May 2004

Steve Davis OBE,
10 Western Road,
Romford, Essex, RM1 3JT,
England

Dear Steve,

You have won over seventy snooker titles. You appear regularly and wittily on the telly. Now you are ready for icon status! With this one simple idea, your reputation will soar way above the realms of 'Steve Davis Plays Chess' – without resorting to the tantrums of Alex Higgins or the bed-hopping of Tony Knowles!

Just change your name from "Steve Davis" to "Steve Davis!" Yes, with an exclamation mark! It demands attention! Imagine the impact on your snooker commentary! And in magazine articles about you! Particularly in "Hello!"! And when playing matches on the telly, they can overlay your pots with Batman-style words like "Pow!" and "Ker-Blam!"

And don't use inferior punctuation! An apostrophe ("Steve D'avis") will make people think that you like "Hear'say". An asterisk ("St*ve Davis") is a dilemma: "B*witched" wore fetching dungarees but "'Nsync" are now "*N Sync". So whenever tempted to stray from the trusted "!", just ask who you really want to be: the mediocre 1980s popsters "a-Ha" or the BAFTA award-winning "Alan Partridge... Ah-Haaaa!"

Anyway, that's my idea!

Please send me a signed photo!

Yours sincerely,

George Andrews

Mr George Andrews

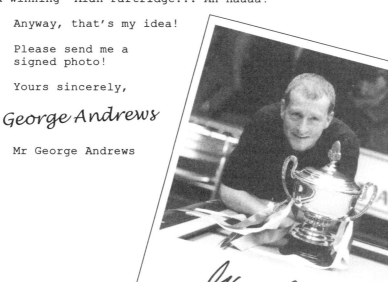

Steve Davis OBE

Absurdly Yours
THE Michael Nugent LETTERS

PART FOUR

PREVIOUS PRANKS

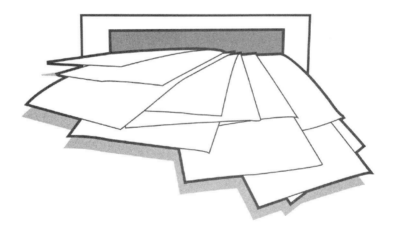

"...We have proof that, since August, highly charged marine life and nuclear barrels have been washed ashore on Sandymount Strand. Every night, Corporation officials take them away and store them in a warehouse in Tallaght..."

- From a leaflet distributed in Sandymount, April 1st 1986.

EVENING PRESS (1982)
THE KISSING IN
PUBLIC DEBATE

Letters to the Editor
The Evening Press
Jan-Feb 1982

KISSING IN PUBLIC

As we enter another new year, I feel I really must put pen to paper about the scandalous decline in the moral standards of the people of Ireland.

Where is all of the Christianity that was so abundant when the Holy Father set foot on Irish soil not so many years ago? Where are the saints and scholars?

I walked from my home to the city centre not so long ago and, as I reached town, not only was I appalled at the amount of perverts that were kissing each other in public, but I could not bring myself to look at the half-naked sinners that adorned the rags that pass as Sunday papers.

God be with the days when you knew it was safe to send your son to school without thinking he would spend his time talking to his friends in the yard about homosexuals, contraception and communists.

People of Ireland repent today, and make 1982 a year that will be remembered for the right reasons — let us love and serve God as we did in the good old days.

ANGELA LAYNE (Mrs)
Swords Road, Swords.

In an Ireland of another era, this was Michael Nugent's first prank letter. It sparked a month-long letters-page debate, plus radio comments and articles in other papers. Sample extracts:

For: "May I add my wholehearted support to Mrs Layne regarding the disgusting displays of kissing in public. Everything today in Ireland is geared towards unholy sex. Scantily-clad females brazenly project themselves from every shop in the land. God be with the days, not too long gone, when pornography was an unknown word to the Irish people."

Against: "What is perverse about kissing? Not being a 'Christian' by Mrs Layne's standards, but having the highest respect for the Pope, he spent quite a lot of time here kissing people in public."

For: "It does Mrs Layne credit that this comparatively mild, though disgusting, public display shocks her. This form of depravity is now common on the streets of our capital city. But I have heard of worse flouting of public morality in parked cars in my area. Birching would be too good for these perverts."

Against: "I hasten to assure Mrs Layne that the schoolyards of the countryside apart from Swords are filled with sanguine thoughts of becoming Christian Brothers and nuns while reading the Messenger and Our Boys."

KISSING: MRS LAYNE REPLIES

Having read numerous replies to my letter (EP 11/1/82), I feel morally bound to add another contribution to the debate.

While I am glad to see so many people support my stand for decency, and indeed support the birching of these perverts, it is a sad reflection on the youth of today that so many others are prepared to defend and encourage perversion in letters to the press.

It does not surprise me to learn that contraceptives are distributed in schools if these letters are anything to go by.

And there is even an accusation (EP 18/1/82) that Our Lord was a communist, but this is irrelevant as the writer is a self-confessed atheist. Indeed, I am shocked that a national Irish newspaper would even print a letter from a person such as this.

And some of these people do not sign their names, but then what can you expect when our Lord Mayor Alexis Fitzgerald is openly dating Mary Flaherty TD when they should be helping run the country. Some example to the youth of today these are.

It seems we are nearer the clutches of Satan than I believed before, but if we repent and change our lifestyles now I am sure we can still be redeemed. like our correspondent from Ballybrack, I am optimistic.

ANGELA LAYNE (Mrs)
Swords Road, Swords.

For: "In its recently published report, the World Health Organisation single out kissing as being one of the major causes of tooth decay. Yet this is but one of the many ill effects of kissing: consider mouth ulcers and venereal disease as prominent examples. These, though seemingly facetious, are rather serious consequences of such a paltry action as kissing."

Against: "The UCD Geography Society has conducted a survey of student opinion. Here are the results: (1) Do you believe kissing in public is immoral? Yes 3%, No 97%. (2) Do you kiss in public? Yes 76%, No 24%. (3) Would you openly discuss the following? Homosexuality: Yes 92%, No 8%. Contraception: Yes 92%, No 8%. Communism: Yes 96%, No 4%."

From the office of Archbishop Ryan of Dublin: "A letter entitled 'Kissing in Public' by Mrs Angela Layne has aroused some considerable comment. One reader makes the point that topics such as homosexuality and contraception are included in the post-primary religious education programme approved by the Catholic Hierarchy. This comment, while substantially correct, seems to have caused some confusion. I would be anxious to point out that what is taught is the teaching of the Catholic Church."

From a Feb 1982 Sunday World article titled 'Less O' Your Lip!': "Douse yourself in holy water! Light bonfires the length and breadth of the land! Cluster together and say a rosary — salvation is at hand! Ever since that Layne woman wrote to the evening paper about kissin' in public, we've been on the move. That vile and communistic practice will be stamped out, and soon..."

JOB APPLICATION (1986)
STILL A FUNNY OLD GAME

In 1985, amid a flurry of media speculation, two senior FAI men drove around England in a hired car. They were looking for people who would consider applying for the job of Ireland soccer manager.

The hype peaked when the media found a more local applicant...

Irish Soccer Manager? I'm Your Man!

The latest Applicant for the position of Irish soccer manager says he is willing to take on the job three days a week for £70 — the equivalent of an AnCO allowance.

He will try to get his local park converted into an international stadium, using the trees as goalposts, and his neighbour's upstairs bedrooms as cost-effective directors' boxes.

Mike Nugent, a graphic designer from Willow Park Grove in Dublin, made his application in writing to the FAI last week. He cited his credentials as having played three games for Willow Park Wanderers ...

20 January 1986

Dear FAI,

    I would like to apply for the still-vacant job of Ireland national football manager. While not intensely involved in competitive football so far this decade, my record during the early to mid seventies shows that my appointment would be a fitting end to the dignified race for this important job.

    Please find enclosed my curriculum vitae. I look forward to hearing from you.

    Yours sincerely,

Michael Nugent

Michael Nugent

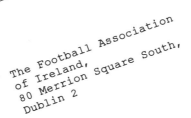

The Football Association
of Ireland,
80 Merrion Square South,
Dublin 2

CURRICULUM VITAE OF MICHAEL NUGENT
IN SUPPORT OF JOB APPLICATION
FOR IRELAND FOOTBALL MANAGER

RELEVANT EXPERIENCE

- I played three games for Willow Park Wanderers U-11 side and nearly scored a goal in an U-13 five-a-side competition in Riversdale Sports Club in June 1972;

- I shook hands with Turlough O'Connor after the 1976 FAI Cup Final between Bohemians and Drogheda United at Dalymount Park;

- I got Derek Dougan's autograph after the 1973 match at Lansdowne Road between Brazil and a Shamrock Rovers All-Ireland selection (the Doog's car also ran over my foot in the carpark, effectively ending my playing career);

- I watched quite a lot of English football on the telly around the time that Leeds United used to come second in everything.

PERSONAL DETAILS

- Although I was born in Ireland, I will be as dedicated and committed to the cause of Irish football as would anyone born in a more appropriate country. I have lived in Éire all of my life, and I have many friends here. I have also picked up enough 'cockneyese' from watching 'Minder' to feel at ease with our second-generation stars.

PLANS FOR THE JOB

- I have devised a deceptively innovative strategy: in each game that we play, we will score more goals than the other team. This means we will win every match, something no manager to date has been able to guarantee.

- I will solve the McCarthy-O'Leary-Lawrenson problem by recalling the 1973 Bohemians central defensive partnership of Johnny Fullam and Joe Burke.

- Obviously Brian if I get the job the lads will be over the parrot and will give 110% and anything else is a bonus and football is still a funny old game Brian obviously.

The FAI appointed Jack Charlton by accident. Bob Paisley got 9 votes out of 18; Liam Tuohy, John Giles and Charlton 3 each. After Tuohy and Giles were eliminated, one voter switched sides and Charlton won by 10 votes to 8.

APRIL FOOLS' DAY (1986) SANDYMOUNT STRAND

On April 1st 1986, Gay Byrne was "arrested" on his morning radio show. The hoax made page one of the early editions of the Evening Herald.

By the later editions, it had been knocked off the front page by a more elaborate hoax on Sandymount Strand...

April fool... with a message

An elaborate April Fools' Day stunt involving radiation warnings and space-suited men on a Dublin beach had a more serious side to it today.

A group of pranksters first handed out thousands of leaflets in Sandymount as part of a hoax anti-Sellafield nuclear processing plant campaign.

Then the April First jokers even went as far as to arrive on the beach dressed up in space suits armed with an array of science fiction equipment.

Sellafield protest: Page three.

Gaybo "arrested" on his radio show: Page seven.

THE LEAFLETS

Very early on April 1st 1986, from 2 to 5 in the morning, a team of 18 people delivered 2,500 leaflets to houses in Sandymount and surrounding areas. From 7 in the morning, another 2,000 leaflets were distributed to commuters in Dublin city centre.

The leaflets informed local residents that the Sellafield Nuclear Action Group (SNAG) were testing Sandymount Strand for radiation.

The operation was planned with the aid of a local postman, who provided street maps warning of houses with dogs to avoid waking any residents. The team deflected the queries of local Garda patrols with improbable reasons for their presence.

THE TESTING

From nine a.m. to noon, three men in chemical suits tested the strand for radiation. They wore toilet seats around their necks.

Michael Nugent carried an electronic box that went beep, Dan McGuinness waved an extended toilet-cleaning rod, and Gerard Nugent planted flags in the strand whenever the box went beep.

Many residents, heeding the leaflets, stayed home. Others came down to the strand, some wearing scarves, to encourage the testers. When questioned about the radiation levels, the testers would say "15.74 megageigerhertz". The only person to notice the toilet seats around the testers' necks was a child.

RADIATION TESTING TODAY ON SANDYMOUNT STRAND

9 A.M. TO 12 NOON, TUESDAY 1st APRIL 1986

To Sandymount Residents & All Citizens

As you know, the Irish Sea is the most radioactive in the world. We have proof that, since August, highly charged marine life and nuclear barrels have been washed ashore on Sandymount Strand. Every night, Corporation officials take them away and store them in a warehouse in Tallaght.

We believe that radiation has now reached 6.3 units per thousand, more than three times the legally acceptable limit. This morning we will be testing the strand for exact levels, and examining the feasibility of counter-screening the radiation through the use of lead oxide.

How YOU Can Support The Tests

▶ Ideally, stay indoors and stock up on fresh drinking water before 8 a.m.

▶ Please do not fill baths; other residents will also need water.

▶ If you must go out, please wear a scarf over your face within a mile of the strand.

▶ If you do go out, please do not interfere with the testers or their equipment.

▶ Start a petition, and join your local residents association.

▶ Contact the media and your public reps (use the phone numbers overleaf).

Thank You For Your Help — The S.N.A.G.

THE OFFICIAL ORGAN OF THE CCCP · VOL I ISSUE 1 JULY 1991

MAJORITY ETHOS

MARRIAGE, NOT SEX · JOBS, NOT CONDOMS · FAITH, NOT SODOMY

HOPEFUL START FOR CCCP

Gloinn Mac Tíre chronicles the conception of a fledgling moral crusade

A clarion call to action was recently put to various Irish Bishops and legislators.

A letter praised the launch of both Christian Solidarity and the Christian Principles Party and called for the formation of a Coordinating Committee for Christianity in Politics.

"Pope Leo XII, while supporting the British in Ireland, outlined a healthy and active role for the Church in politics," it read, "and Pope John Paul II has brought this noble crusade up to date.

"Most Fianna Fáil families are decent people. There

Archbishop Connell: *"Contact the Knights of Saint Columbanus"*

Sean Doherty: *"Anxious to hear views of other Oireachtas members"*

Bishop Comiskey: *"Deserving a response from Bishops as a body"*

may be Christian minorities in the secular Bruton and Socialist parties. We must now unite, without of course becoming Unitarians. Then we can tackle the cross-channel tragedy of separated spouses remarrying, stop our

children becoming pregnant before we can protect them from sex education, and reverse the satanic tide of student-activist-inspired discussion of abortion."

Initial response has been positive to this plea *...contd*

...contd

Across:
1 Godless TD, friend of the discredited Sandinistas of Nicaragua (7)
5 Former Communist revolutionary from Ballyfermot, now a popular light entertainment radio presenter and inventor of the Karaoke phenomenon (5)
6 And behold the opposite of 'Hi' (2)
8 The amount of Workers Party members facing eternal retribution (3)
9 Christian Principles Party slogan (4,4)
12 Protestant King responsible for Battle of the Boyne (5)
14 Liberal legislator and probable sympathiser with 12 across (5,4)

Down:
1 Final destination of 1 and 14 across (4)
2 The ultimate Judge of fornicators, condom-mongers and sodomites (3)
3 The Pope is certainly this, to be sure, to be sure (10)
4 The Government's condom legislation is certainly this (5)
7 Popular beef cube used in cooking (3)
9 More than one Saviour could lead to this cricket ground (5)
10 We've had enough of this - - -th on our TV screens, says Mary Whitehouse (3)
11 Organisation that should promote the correct role of women in Ireland (3)
13 Ulster does not say this (3)

Answers Across: 1 Higgins; 5 Duffy; 6 Lo; 8 All; 9 Love Life; 12 Billy; 14 Shane Ross;
Down: 1 Hell; 2 God; 3 Infallible; 4 Folly; 7 Oxo; 9 Lords; 10 Fil; 11 ICA; 13 Yes.

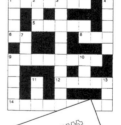

In 1991 Gloinn Mac Tíre (Michael Nugent) and Eoin Ó Ceallaigh (Arthur Mathews) wrote to bishops and politicians seeking support for the new Coordinating Committee for Christianity in Politics (CCCP). Its newsletter was Majority Ethos.

Cathaoirleach Sheanad Éireann
Teach Laighean
Baile Átha Cliath 2

Cathaoirleach of Seanad Éireann
Leinster House
Dublin 2

Senator Seán Doherty, Cathaoirleach of the Seanad

Dear Mr. Mac Tíre,

Thank you for your letter and what you propose is certainly an interesting idea. Naturally, I am anxious to know if you have been in contact with any other members of the Oireachtas. If so, who are they, so I could hear their views and seek to establish what they have in mind.

Yours sincerely,

Seán Doherty
Cathaoirleach

Telephone: 373732

ARCHBISHOP'S HOUSE

DUBLIN 9

Dear Mr Mac Tíre,

Archbishop Connell has asked me to reply to your letter. The Archbishop appreciates very much your concern regarding aspects of Irish society. He has noted the suggestion you have made in your letter. However, you will appreciate that the Archbishop cannot involve himself in political initiatives of the kind you are suggesting. For this reason, may I propose that you contact organisations which have as their object the promotion and extension of the faith in all areas of life. One such group which has experience in this area is the Order of the Knights of Saint Columbanus. I hope that this suggestion is of assistance.

Rev Michael O'Kelly
Secretary

FROM DEAR JOHN (1993)
BRING BACK
CJ HAUGHEY

Letter sent to Charles
J Haughey in Feb 1993

*(From 'Dear John: The John
Mackay Letters', Michael
Nugent & Sam Smyth, 1993)*

Dear Mr Haughey,

I am writing as a citizen of Ireland about a matter of vital national importance. As our very currency stumbles through multiple self-inflicted political minefields, it is becoming increasingly clear that you should never have vacated the Taoiseachship. I plead with you, Mr Haughey, to reconsider your too-hasty retirement. 'Consensus' Reynoldsite politics may seem superficially 'reasonable', but you and I know that progress depends on the unreasonable man.

Yes, of course, you were opposed by an inconsequential rabble of small, petty people, obsessed with insignificant so-called 'scandals' of a decade ago, and burning inside with jealousy of your political wisdom and courage, your proud Irish republicanism, your patronage of the arts and the Bishops, your sense of your place in history — your very political essence, Mr Haughey, to which they could not aspire and so conspired to destroy, scrambling feverishly to add their fingerprints to the dagger that was Doherty's.

You, Mr Haughey, were not merely a political Houdini but a modern European Cúchulainn, unfazed by 'scandals' that would have ended the career of a mere political mortal. You owe it to yourself and the nation to return to active politics, biding your time with dignity until your invisible successor is seen for the visionless pet-food manufacturer that he is.

I and some colleagues are planning to launch a non-party-political 'Bring Back Charles J Haughey' campaign. We have a sizeable nest-egg available, and we do not need any 'seed capital' from you. Do we need your formal endorsement, or should that come after the launch? We bow to your wisdom.

Yours sincerely,

John Mackay

Mr John Mackay

Mr Charles J Haughey,
Kinsaley,
County Dublin

KINSALEY COUNTY DUBLIN

2nd March 1993

Dear John,

Thank you very much for your interesting letter of the 17th February.

I think it would be helpful if we were to meet and discuss your suggestion.

If you agree, perhaps you would contact Marie Sheehan at *******
to arrange something mutually convenient.

I greatly appreciate the kind sentiments you have expressed and look forward to talking to you.

With kindest regards,

Yours sincerely,

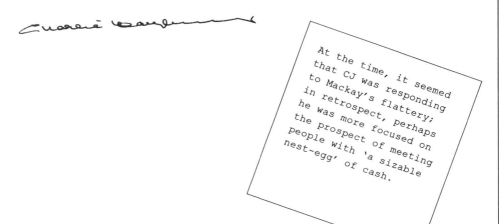

At the time, it seemed that CJ was responding to Mackay's flattery; in retrospect, perhaps he was more focused on the prospect of meeting people with 'a sizable nest-egg' of cash.

Second of three letters sent to Bertie Ahern in 1993; he finally replied to a further reminder two months later

(From 'Dear John: The John Mackay Letters', Michael Nugent & Sam Smyth, 1993)

Dear Mr Ahern,

You are growing apace in stature as the toast of drawing room Dublin 4 following your heroic devaluation of the punt. However, in the midst of this organised chaos, either the postal system has gone awry or some light-fingered lad in your very office has pocketed £5 which I sent to you over THREE MONTHS AGO.

My niece was preparing a UCD thesis entitled 'Politics and People', and I had asked you to verify the authenticity of two anecdotes for inclusion. She has now drafted the relevant sections thusly:

- "They call him the anorak man, but he does not hang around with hoods. On boxing day itself he braves the snow to hand-deliver Christmas greetings to his grateful constituents. Bah, humbug, moan his opponents, but Bertie delivers, both literally and metaphorically."
  (page 43, para 4)

- "Accused that his canvassers were misleading voters by claiming there were no health cuts, an unfazed Bertie simply laughed: 'Ah sure God love them, they're not familiar with the details'. The hostility was defused; as always, it was Bertie and the voter against everyone else."
  (page 62, para 2)

Bertie, you are a busy man, so a brief authorisation to include the anecdotes will suffice. No need for a sworn enquiry on the fiver, though it would be nice to know that it has reached its intended destination. If it hasn't, please let me know and I will send another by return of post.

Yours sincerely,

John Mackay

Mr John Mackay

Mr Bertie Ahern TD,
Minister for Finance,
Department of Finance,
Merrion Street,
Dublin 2

OIFIG AN AIRE AIRGEADAIS
(OFFICE OF THE MINISTER FOR FINANCE)
BAILE ÁTHA CLIATH 2.
(DUBLIN 2)

30th July 1993

Dear John,

I would like to thank you for forwarding towards the Fianna Fáil party your kind donation.

With regard to the quotes, unfortunately I cannot recall the incidents in question and therefore I cannot verify them.

Best wishes,

Yours sincerely,

Bertie

Bertie Ahern TD
Minister for Finance

Practising for the Mahon Tribunal eleven years later, Bertie first ignores questions about an informal meeting and a missing political donation, then eventually replies that he can not recall the incidents.

Emigration Control Platform

13 January 1998

Dear Ms Ní Chónaill,

May we congratulate you on the formation of your new group, the Immigration Control Platform, and your admirable aim of keeping foreign people out of Ireland. Our complementary aim is to keep Irish people out of foreign countries. Our immediate goals include:

- The immediate repatriation of all 70 million Irish emigrants and an apology from the President to every nation that we have contaminated with our culture.
- The closure of all Irish airports except Shannon, which would be turned into a ring-fenced cultural theme park for short-stay wealthy tourists.
- The return of the de Valera family to New York or Spain, to be replaced in Ireland by the Kennedy, Reagan, Clinton and Castro families.
- The above copper-fastened by a Constitutional Amendment, with voting restricted to people with pale skin, red hair and freckles.

We look forward to our two groups working together to win the important fight for national purity.

Yours sincerely,

Michael Nugent

Anne Holliday

Michael Nugent
Anne Holliday

Ms Áine Ní Chónaill,
Chairperson,
Immigration Control Platform,
P.O. Box 6469, Dublin 2,
Ireland

Absurdly Yours
THE Michael Nugent LETTERS

PART FIVE

P.S.

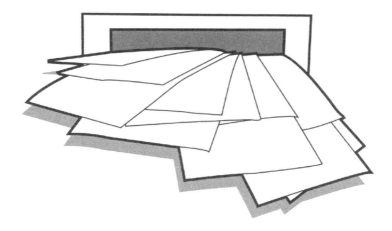

"...Gerry Ryan, moral decline,
condoms, marijuana,
all kinds of everything
make me vote for Dana..."

- From a proposed
   Presidential campaign
   song sent to Dana.

8 September 2004

The Chief Executive,
Irish Pharmaceutical
Healthcare Association

Dear Chief Executive,

I am writing about a sensitive matter which I know you will treat with appropriate discretion.

I live with my elderly mother, who has in the past couple of years developed a minor addiction to the potassium iodate tablets distributed by the Government to protect us from Sellafield.

Health Minister Micheál Martin has advised me to get some pharmaceutical placebos to satisfy her concerns.

Can you direct me towards any placebos that are shaped like, and taste like, potassium iodate tablets, and that could be supplied in similar packaging?

Also, as our neighbours have been supplying mother with their potassium iodate tablets, and none of us now have any left, we would need placebos that would work in the same way as potassium iodate, just in case (God forbid) there is an actual emergency.

Thank you for your assistance.

Yours sincerely,

Bernard Campbell

Mr Bernard Campbell

The Chief Executive,
Irish Pharmaceutical
Healthcare Association,
Franklin House,
140 Pembroke Road,
Dublin 4

IRISH PHARMACEUTICAL HEALTHCARE ASSOCIATION

15th October 2004

Dear Mr. Campbell

I refer to your letters of the 8th September and 4th October which have been passed to me.

The Irish Pharmaceutical Healthcare Association has no information regarding the potassium iodate tablets or suitable placebos and regret therefore that we cannot help you in this instance.

Yours sincerely,

Vivienne Hough

Vivienne Hough
Communications Executive

Tragically, Mr Campbell fails in his final attempt to ensure that his neighbourhood (still without any of the precious iodine tablets) is safe if Sellafield explodes.

8 September 2004

Dear Dana,

Our family is delighted that you are planning another campaign for the presidency. We will certainly be out knocking on doors for you again. So here is some money that our children raised at a sale of work selling 'All Kinds of Everything', and an idea to give your campaign that little something extra.

My mother is a veteran of many John Player Tops of the Towns competitions. And last weekend, she gathered the family around the piano to make a list of all that is wrong with Ireland, which she turned into this modern variation of 'All Kinds of Everything'...

Chancers, financiers, John Bowman's ties,
European super-states, Vincent Browne's sighs,
Gerry Ryan, moral decline, condoms, marijuana,
All kinds of everything make me vote for Dana.

Liberals and lesbians, Michael Lowry's charm,
Telly Bingo, Bertie-speak, Celebrity Farm,
Michael D, RTÉ, immigrants from Ghana,
All kinds of everything make me vote for Dana.

Summertime, wintertime, waiting for mañana,
Monday, Tuesday, every day, we'll vote for Dana.

What do you think? It conveys serious points, in a light Christy Moore sort of way, and could get below the radar of the liberal media bias. Please feel free to record it and use it, as they say, on the doorsteps. We will certainly be singing it in our house to celebrate your ascent to the Presidency.

Yours sincerely,

Damhnait Evans

Mrs Damhnait Evans

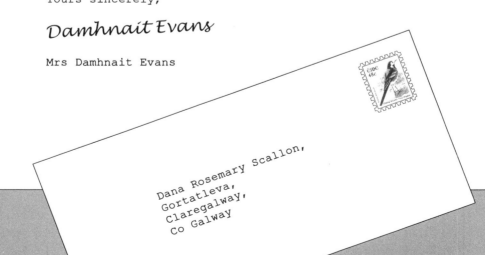

Dana Rosemary Scallon,
Gortatleva,
Claregalway,
Co Galway

Dana Rosemary Scallon
Gortatleva, Claregalway, Co. Galway

20/10/04

Dear Damhnait,

Thank you very much for your lovely letter and for the very thoughtful donation. Please tell your children that I really appreciate it and I know that it took a lot of time and effort for them to raise that amount.

It was very disturbing that the main political parties prevented a democratic election for the Presidency, but no doubt you have been following the EU Constitution with interest. The upcoming referendum will certainly be an opportunity for you and your family to speak up in defence of our national sovereignty. Thank God for people like you.

On a lighter note, I just couldn't stop laughing when I read the lyrics written by your mother. I can see why she's been so successful in the Tops of the Towns competitions. She's very clever. I will be taking a copy of them to my mum; I know she'll have a good laugh when she reads them.

Again, many thanks and please keep in touch,

God bless,

Dana

4 October 2004

Ms Ursula Halligan,
The Political Party,
TV3

Dear Ursula,

Congratulations on your new show. My wife and I found it very interesting. Don't you think that Willie O'Dea looks less like Groucho Marx now that he has ditched the glasses? Seeing you also reminded us that we had written to you a while ago, asking if you could settle a small family bet. Perhaps it got lost in the post.

Basically, my wife is convinced that you are related to Angela Lansbury, who played Jessica Fletcher in the literary detective series 'Murder, She Wrote'. She bases this on your uncanny physical similarity, and the fact that Ms Lansbury lived for some time in Ballycotton, County Cork. So, we wondered ...

Also, here is a new idea, based on the popularity of reality television shows. Why don't you front a reality series called 'Murder, She Reported', in which you would both report on and try to solve unsolved Irish murders? If it worked, you could expand it and solve murders in every country where the original series was shown.

Anyway, please let us know who is right.

Yours sincerely,

Tim O'Reilly

Mr Tim O'Reilly

Ms Ursula Halligan,
The Political Party, TV3,
Westgate Business Park,
Ballymount,
Dublin 24

Political Correspondents' Room,
2nd Floor,
Leinster House,
Dublin 2

23rd October, 2004

Dear Mr O'Reilly,

Please accept my deepest apologies for the delay in replying to your two
letters. Unfortunately, as I am based in Leinster House, post that is sent to
me addressed to TV3 in Ballymount often takes ages to reach me.

But I am so glad I eventually received your two wonderful letters because
they gave me such a laugh. You're not the first one to spot the physical
similarity between the great Angela Lansbury and myself. I've been teased
about it since my teenage years and am regularly called 'Jessica' for fun by
certain people.

I hope that you won't be too disappointed (or lose too much money on your
bet) when I tell you that (as far as I know) I am not related to Ms Lansbury.

However, I love your idea for a new show — although somehow I don't
think that *'Murder, She Reported'* would be a runner with my TV3
bosses !!! ☺

I am also flattered and grateful that you took the time to write to me to
explore my lineage and hope that yourself and your wife continue to watch
The Political Party.

Yours sincerely,

Ursula Halligan (Jessica!)

Ursula Halligan

21 September 2004

Mrs Teresa Heinz Kerry,
Chairman, Howard Heinz Endowment,
Pittsburgh, USA

Dear Mrs Heinz Kerry,

I know your husband is a busy man, but I wrote to him nearly two months ago, saying that I want to support his campaign. Could you maybe remind him over breakfast tomorrow? Just tell him from me: "Three words... Bring! It! On!"

I also suggested that he be photographed with Kerry McFadden, holding a newspaper report of Kerry winning that television reality show set in the Australian bush. The headline would read: "Three words... Kerry Beats Bush!"

I used to live in Boston and I may be back there later this summer to help. If not, next year to celebrate. When John is President and you are the new Hillary (without the 'pain').

Also, can you please ask him to send me some campaign badges? I have badges for every Democratic candidate since JFK.

Yours sincerely,

Jack Thomas

Mr Jack Thomas

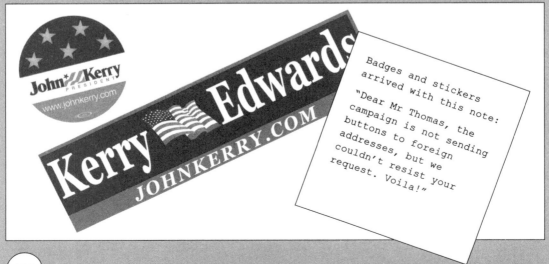

Badges and stickers arrived with this note: "Dear Mr Thomas, the campaign is not sending buttons to foreign addresses, but we couldn't resist your request. Voila!"

TOP FIFTEEN PRANKS OF ALL TIME

 15 **Bush's IQ "inferior to average man's", concludes independent study**

In July 2001, an independent think-tank located in Scranton, Pennsylvania, declared George W Bush as the least intelligent US President of the past fifty years. The Lovenstein Institute rated the last twelve Presidents by psychological factors, scholarly achievements, ability to speak clearly and writings unaided by staff. They concluded that, with the exception of Richard Nixon, Democratic Presidents were more intelligent than Republican ones.

IQ	President	Party
182	William J Clinton	Dem
175	James E Carter	Dem
174	John F Kennedy	Dem
155	Richard M Nixon	Rep
147	Franklin D Roosevelt	Dem
132	Harry Truman	Dem
126	Lyndon B Johnson	Dem
122	Dwight D Eisenhower	Rep
121	Gerald Ford	Rep
105	Ronald Reagan	Rep
99	George HW Bush	Rep
91	George W Bush	Rep

Newspapers around the world covered the story. Russia's *Pravda* led with "Bush's IQ Inferior to Average Man's." When Bush visited Britain, *The Guardian* wished "a very warm welcome to George Walker Bush, with news from his homeland that he is now officially the dimmest president in 50 years… the poor chap scores an abysmal 91." The New Zealand *Southland Times* and the German *Bild* also reported the study, before research showed it to be a spoof item from the website *linkydinky.com*. *The Guardian*'s Mathew Norman, on realising the paper's error, wrote: "Ah, research, we remember that. We've let Scranton down, we've let President Bush down, we've let *The Guardian* down, but most of all we've let ourselves down. Poor show."

 14 **Russian government to seek foreign currency by selling Lenin's body**

In November 1991, shortly after the collapse of the Soviet Union, the Russian economy was in a perilous state. ABC News and *USA Today* both reported that the Russian government were seeking foreign currency by selling the embalmed body of Vladimir Lenin. Bidding would start at $15 million. After Russia denounced the report as an "impudent lie", it was revealed that it began as a prank story in American business magazine *Forbes FYI*.

13 Enraged customer responds to $250 bill with internet email campaign

The following story has been widely circulated by email. A woman and her daughter had cookies at a Neiman Marcus Café in Dallas. When she asked to see their recipe, the waitress said she could buy it for two fifty. She agreed, but was shocked when she found that her next VISA statement had a charge of $250 for the recipe. The department store refused to refund the money, saying that she had already seen the recipe. So the woman got her revenge by posting the recipe for free on the Internet, asking people to circulate it to as many people as they could. Variations of this hoax have been circulating for decades, with various companies being the target of the story, but the Neiman Marcus one is the most common, and was the most widely circulated. Neiman Marcus responded by publishing its own cookie recipe on its website, thus taking advantage of the publicity generated by the hoax. For a while, the Neiman Marcus website gave 'Cookie Recipe' almost as much prominence as investor relations and career opportunities.

> **The Hoax Recipe**
>
> 2 cups butter; 4 cups flour; 2 tsp. baking soda; 2 cups sugar; 5 cups blended oatmeal (measure oatmeal and blend in a blender to a fine powder); 24 oz. chocolate chips; 2 cups brown sugar; 1 tsp. salt; 1 - 8 oz. Hershey Bar (grated); 4 eggs; 2 tsp. baking powder; 2 tsp. vanilla; 3 cups chopped nuts (your choice, but we liked pecans best)
>
> Cream the butter and both sugars. Add eggs and vanilla; mix together with flour, oatmeal, salt, baking powder, and soda. Add chocolate chips, Hershey Bar and nuts. Roll into balls and place two inches apart on a cookie sheet. Bake for 10 minutes at 375 degrees. Makes 112 cookies.

12 New technology to alert consumers to out-of-date cola, says Virgin Cola

On April 1st 1996, Richard Branson's Virgin Cola issued a consumer safety alert. It announced that the company had evolved a new technology for the cans in which the cola was sold. When the cola went past its expiration date, a chemical would be activated, the cola would react with the metal of the can, and the can would turn a bright blue. With cautious consumers avoiding bright blue cola cans, rivals Pepsi were less than impressed: they had just launched a new range of bright blue Pepsi cans.

11 Census shows that seven in every thousand Britons are Jedi Knights

In 2001, the UK Office of National Statistics published an official list of religions as part of its computer analysis of the 2001 census. Listed among the religions was Jedi Knights. It was the first time that the UK census had asked about religion, and Star Wars fans had responded with an email campaign asking people to describe themselves as Jedi Knights. Nearly 400,000 people in England and Wales did so, and 'Jedi Knights' was duly assigned its own census code (896).

Areas with most Jedi Knights, 2001		
Area	**Jedis**	**%**
Brighton and Hove UA	6,480	2.6
Oxford	2,742	2.0
Wandsworth	5,024	1.9
Cambridge	2,022	1.9
Southampton UA	3,944	1.8
Lambeth	4,745	1.8
Exeter	1,942	1.7
Reading UA	2,500	1.7
Bristol; City of UA	6,642	1.7
Islington	2,904	1.7
England and Wales	**390,127**	**0.7**

However, the official census website groups them together with those who "stated that they had no religion: this category included agnostics, atheists, heathens and those who wrote Jedi Knight."

10 Isaac Bickerstaff predicts the death of fellow astrologer John Partridge

London astrologer John Partridge was enraged when *Predictions for the Year 1708,* by rival astrologer Isaac Bickerstaff, foretold that Partridge would die "by a raging fever" at exactly 11.00 pm on March 29. Partridge denounced the claim as a hoax, but on March 30 Bickerstaff published a eulogy proclaiming Partridge had indeed died on the appointed day, only four hours earlier than predicted. News reached London the following morning, April 1st, and Partridge was woken when his sexton called to check funeral details. He then continually encountered puzzled stares from everybody who had heard of this well-timed death. A furious Partridge published a new pamphlet insisting that he was still alive, to which Bickerstaff responded with another pamphlet saying that he must be dead, as nobody alive could have published the rubbish that Partridge had in his previous almanac. Bickerstaff was actually Jonathan Swift, later Dean of Saint Patrick's Cathedral in Dublin, who was upset by Partridge's attacks on the Church of England. His prank had the desired result. The humiliated Partridge lost all public credibility, and eventually had to stop publishing his almanacs.

9   "The events depicted in this film took place in Minnesota in 1987"

In 1996, the Coen Brothers' cult movie *Fargo*, in which a string of murders culminate in a body being put through a wood-chipper, opened with this line: "This is a true story. The events depicted in this film took place in Minnesota in 1987. At the request of the survivors, the names have been changed. Out of respect for the dead, the rest has been told exactly as it occurred." Many reviewers repeated this claim, and news reporters spent months trying to source the original story. But *Fargo* is not a true story. When William H Macey was cast in the lead role, he is said to have asked the Coens if he should research the original incident. They told him that everything in the movie is fictional. He replied that the script starts with a claim that it is true. They said, yes, that claim is in the movie, and everything in the movie is fictional.

8   Astronomical event enables people to float in air, says Patrick Moore

On April 1st 1976, astronomer Patrick Moore told listeners to BBC Radio 2 about a unique astronomical event that morning. At exactly 9.47 am, he said, Pluto would pass behind Jupiter, causing a temporary realignment of gravity that would counter the effect of gravity on earth. If listeners jumped in the air at exactly 9.47, he said, they would experience a strange floating sensation. Hundreds of listeners phoned in to say they had experienced it, with one woman claiming that twelve people had floated around her room, and another that she had risen so fast that she had hit her head on the ceiling.

7   "Perhaps there is intelligent life out there after all…"

In 1993, a crop circle of symmetrically flattened rye appeared in a field outside Johannesburg, South Africa. Because it was the first time the phenomenon had reached South Africa, there followed weeks of media speculation about whether a UFO had created it. Finally, somebody noticed that the rye had been flattened in the shape of the BMW logo. An ad agency had created the circle as part of a TV campaign for BMW, which was later broadcast with the tagline "perhaps there is intelligent life out there after all…"

6 Mild winter causes very high spaghetti harvest in Switzerland, says BBC

On April 1st 1957, BBC current affairs programme *Panorama* told viewers that a mild winter in southern Switzerland had led to a much bigger than usual spaghetti harvest. Host David Dimbleby gave a deadpan commentary over scenes of a family from Ticino in Switzerland picking strings of spaghetti from trees and gathering them in baskets. He explained that the bumper crop had also been helped by the absence that year of the impressive-sounding spaghetti weevil. Many rang in to ask how they could grow their own spaghetti trees. Even Sir Ian Jacob, the BBC's Director General, checked a reference book to see if the story was true.

5 British astronomer discovers winged humanoid man-bats on the moon

In 1835 *The New York* Sun reported that the British astronomer Sir John Herschel had invented a telescope so powerful that he could investigate the insect life on the moon. The paper spent a week running stories on Sir Herschel's discoveries. He had seen unicorns, two-footed beavers and:

> "four successive flocks of large winged creatures, wholly unlike any kind of birds, descending with a slow even motion from the cliffs on the western side, and alighting upon the plain… certainly they were like human beings, for their wings had now disappeared, and their attitude in walking was both erect and dignified… we scientifically denominated them as Vespertilio-homo, or man-bat; they are doubtless innocent and happy creatures, though some of their amusements would but ill comport with our terrestrial notions of decorum."

News of the lunar man-bats spread across America, and for decades afterwards hard-to-believe tales were described as being "moon-hoaxy".

4   20th Annual New York April Fools' Day Parade to take place in 2005

2005 will see the 20th Annual New York April Fools' Day Parade. The 2004 Parade included the Iraqi War Float featuring President Bush showing off Saddam Hussein, the Michael Jackson Giant Bed Float where parents could let their kids ride the length of the parade, the Smokers-only Bar and Restaurant Float and more. The parade does not exist, but press releases each year announcing it have caused most major media outlets to turn up to cover it. The man behind it is Joey Skaggs. In the 1960s, when tourists descended on New York's East Village to photograph hippies, he organised a reciprocal Hippie Bus Tour of Queens. In 1976 he opened a "a cathouse for dogs" where owners could treat their pets to $50-worth of canine sex. After public protest and a subpoena from the District Attorney, he revealed that it was a prank. Since then Skaggs has got media coverage for the Celebrity Sperm Bank, Gypsies Against Stereotypical Propaganda (see picture above), Fish Condos for upwardly mobile guppies, Windsurfing from Hawaii to California, the Fat Squad service where diet commandoes stay with you to ensure that you don't overeat, the Brooklyn Bridge Lottery and much more.

3   Mariah Carey upset by sight of starving children all over the world

In 1996, *The Independent* in London and *The San Francisco Chronicle* were among dozens of publications who quoted singer Mariah Carey as saying: "When I watch TV and see those poor starving kids all over the world, I can't help but cry. I mean, I'd love to be skinny like that, but not with all those flies and death and stuff." But Carey had never said it. It came from a spoof interview in a web publication called *Cupcake*, which was then quoted in the British magazine *Vox*. In reality, Mariah Carey supports a number of charities, and works with the Make a Wish Foundation and Camp Mariah.

2   "A nude horse is a rude horse" says campaigner for clothed animals

In the 1960s, American G Clifford Prout founded the Society for Indecency to Naked Animals (SINA). "A nude horse is a rude horse" was one of its slogans, as it campaigned for the clothing of all animals. Announced on NBC's *Today* show, SINA remained active for years. Prout was actually jazz percussionist and master prankster Alan Abel. During Watergate, he held a press conference to introduce 'Deep Throat', Bernstein and Woodward's

Alan Abel

secret source. At the conference, the pseudo 'Deep Throat' had a row with his 'wife' over going public, and was whisked away in a waiting limo. Later, as 'Omar The Beggar', Abel got massive publicity for his new School for Professional Panhandlers. In 1980 he tricked *The New York Times* into publishing his obituary, then called a press conference to announce that reports of his death were greatly exaggerated. In 1985 he paid a team of people to join the Donohue Show audience and pretend to faint. The rest of the audience fled, leaving Donohue to continue the show in an empty studio. Abel has also run for the US Congress on a manifesto of putting politicians on a commission-only salary and dropping Wednesday to establish a four-day workweek.

1   Airline passengers perturbed at their welcome to Los Angeles

Michael's choice for the top prank of all time:
On April 1st 1992, airline passengers descending into Los Angeles Airport could look out the window and see an 85-foot banner spread on the ground of the nearby Hollywood Park racetrack. In 20-foot high letters, the banner read: "Welcome to Chicago."

Sources for 'Top Fifteen Pranks of All Time' include Re/Search Pranks (Re/Search Publications, 1987), The Book of Brilliant Hoaxes (Simon Rose, 1995), The Museum of Hoaxes (Alex Boese, 2002), and many websites.

INDEX

www.michael-nugent.com